TWENTIETH CENTURY CAESAR

Benito Mussolini

Born: July 29, 1883
Died: April 28, 1945

Son of a blacksmith who was an ardent Socialist,
Mussolini grew up in an atmosphere of political
agitation. He was a teacher for a brief time, then
an editor of various newspapers with strong
Socialist leanings. When World War I was declared, his political point of view changed and he
became an extreme nationalist, even joining
the Italian army. During the troubled postwar
period, he was elected to parliament and organized the blackshirt Fascist party. When Victor
Emmanuel made him premier, he slowly transformed the government into a dictatorship.
Ambitious and ruthless, he had faith in his
destiny to rule Italy and restore it to the power
and splendor of the ancient Roman Empire, see-
ing himself as the new Caesar. The Rome-Berlin
axis, in which he allied himself with Hitler, was
the beginning of his downfall, and led to the way
of all dictators—death at the hands of the people
who had once revered him.

Books by Jules Archer

FRONT-LINE GENERAL
Douglas MacArthur

TWENTIETH CENTURY CAESAR
Benito Mussolini

TWENTIETH CENTURY CAESAR

Benito Mussolini

By

Jules Archer

Julian Messner, Inc. • New York

Published by Julian Messner, Inc.
8 West 40 Street, New York 18

© Copyright 1964 by Jules Archer

Printed in the United States of America
Library of Congress Catalog Card No. 64-20159

To my sons
Mike, Dane and Kerry

Some descriptions of life under Fascism in Italy derive from the author's personal observations during a cycle trip through Europe in 1938. Recollections of the Rome-Berlin Axis days also come from yellowed copies of *Il Lavoro Fascista, Paris-soir* and *The Manchester Guardian*.

The author owes a special debt of gratitude to Mr. George Seldes, distinguished author of *Sawdust Caesar,* and to Mr. Paolo Monelli, author of *Mussolini: The Intimate Life of a Demagogue* (through the courtesy of Miss Evelyn Shrifte of Vanguard Press, Inc.), for permission to refer to significant facts about Mussolini I was able to find in no other sources.

Jules Archer

Pine Plains
New York

CONTENTS

· 1 ·

TROUBLEMAKER

A sharp blow on his temple, delivered without warning, sent the blacksmith's son sprawling against the fieldstone wall of the earth-floored smithy.

"Badate! Be careful!" growled Alessandro Mussolini. "You've let the fire die down. Blow the bellows!"

Large black eyes smoldering with rage, Benito returned to the forge. He was angry at his father, who automatically administered a beating for daydreaming and other sins of a seven-year-old.

Jaw set, he worked the bellows savagely as his father turned the dull crimson horseshoe in the forge, then laid it on the anvil and beat it into shape with powerful blows. Benito watched in reluctant fascination, torn between admiration and hatred.

"Enough for today!" his father grumbled, laying down his hammer. He reached for a bottle on the shelf, bit out the cork and let the sparkling red Sangiovese flow down his throat. At this signal that the day's work had come to an end, Benito raced out of the smithy and through the mountain village, past vats ready for the grape harvest standing outside the old stone house. Heading for a nearby farm field, he joined a circle of boys gazing in wonder at a huge new threshing machine.

After a while, tiring of the spectacle, he discovered an empty wheelbarrow on its side. Gripping its high handles, he tested his seven-year-old strength to see if he could lift and push it.

"Hey, Benito! Want a game with us?"

The boy was Orsi Giacona, son of the bootmaker, almost a head taller and three years older. Flattered, Benito abandoned the wheelbarrow and raced toward Orsi's group. The taller boy suddenly stepped forward and swung at him, landing a punch on his mouth that sent Benito sprawling into a row of grape vines.

"The game is called swap, stupid," Orsi jeered. "I swap my fist for your wheelbarrow!" He raced off with the barrow as the other boys howled with laughter.

Benito thrashed his way out of the vines, lip bleeding, eyes wide with shock and hurt at Orsi's treachery. He fled from the field before the first tears came, but by the time he reached the mossy stone wall near his house he was sobbing bitterly, "Mama . . . Mama . . . "

A powerful fist pinned him against the wall. "Tears are for women," Alessandro Mussolini growled.

"B-but a big boy hit me, Papa—"

"Then go back and teach him never to dare lay a hand on anyone with the name of Mussolini!"

Even more afraid of his father than of Orsi, Benito desperately racked his brains for a way out of his dilemma. A pointed brown stone in the dirt road caught his eye. Prying it out of the earth, he held it like a dagger and raced back to the field, where Orsi was giving another boy a ride in the barrow. Before the bootmaker's son had a chance to defend himself, Benito struck savagely with the pointed rock. He pounded his enemy twice over the ear, then once in the mouth; Orsi fell, screaming at the top of his lungs as he tasted blood. When he fled in terror, the other boys around Benito fell back respectfully.

Fiercely proud, he returned home in great excitement and jubilantly described his revenge to his father. The blacksmith clapped him on the back with the force of a striking hammer.

"*Sia ringraziato il cielo!* Heaven be praised! Now you've learned the first lesson of a man, my son. Never put up with bullying! If you listen to the priests and turn the other cheek, you'll get a slam on that one, too. To win respect always carry a sharp knife and use it when you must!"

So it was that a children's scuffle in an obscure Italian mountain village, that sunswept September day in 1890, began to shape the iron in the soul of a boy who eventually enslaved the Italian nation.

Benito Mussolini, named by his revolution-minded father after Benito Juárez, liberator of Mexico, was born on July 29, 1883, on a high hillside above the village of Dovia in the commune of Predappio. This is the region of northeast Italy known as Romagna; its people are hotheaded, rebellious, warmhearted, and overly fond of wine, women, song and vendettas.

The future dictator of Italy was born in an old stone house which had the smithy on the ground floor, below a room in which his mother attempted to teach school over the ringing of the anvil. The family lived in two rooms on the top floor. For as early as Benito could remember his parents quarreled constantly over the lack of meat for the table. Teaching poor village pupils brought Rosa Mussolini only a pittance, and her husband was much fonder of drinking and Socialist agitation than of making sparks fly profitably under his hammer.

The three Mussolini children—Benito, his brother Arnaldo and little sister Edvige—often went hungry. Dire poverty made Benito, like his father, bitter at those powerful Italians who lived in luxury while so many in the Romagna were on the edge of starvation. Yet at the same time he was deeply envious, determined that someday, somehow, those at the top would have to make room for Benito Mussolini. Years later, when he had made those dreams come true, he recalled grimly, "Hunger is a good teacher. Almost as good as prison and a man's enemies!"

His swarthy, heavyset father was the leading political figure in Dovia, greatly respected because as a youth he had spent three years in jail for having helped the famous Russian anarchist Mikhail Bakunin introduce revolutionary Socialism into Italy. Signor Mussolini's booming voice could be heard holding forth relentlessly against Church and State in the smithy, at the inn, at home. He bullied and whipped his children frequently, convinced this would toughen them for survival in a world he saw as a jungle.

Benito's mother, Rosa, was a gentle, well-educated, long-suffering woman who came from a better family than her husband. Deeply pious, she was grieved by his loudly trumpeted atheism, especially since it kept many parents from sending their children to her school.

Benito adored his mother and began his schooling in her classroom. He took revenge for his unhappiness at home by tormenting the other pupils. Signora Mussolini despaired of getting him to stop crawling underneath the benches to pinch the bare legs of his classmates. After school he would chase girls in the fields, sometimes seizing and kissing them, sometime grabbing their braids and driving them like horses. Hoping to soften her son's aggressive nature, Signora Mussolini scrimped until she could afford to buy a second-hand violin for him, beseeching fiddlers who passed through Dovia to or from nearby fairs to give him lessons.

As the most audacious boy in Dovia, he was the ring-leader of the village's young toughs. Once he led them on a raid of an apple orchard and sent a boy named Piero over the wall and into a tree to shake its branches. The out-raged owner suddenly appeared, gun in hand, and fired point-blank into the tree foliage.

"I'm hit!" Piero screamed. "My God, I'm hit!"

As he fell out of the tree, blood staining the right leg of his trousers, the other boys fled in terror. All except Benito, who shouted bitter curses at them. Then he lifted the weeping Piero onto his shoulder and carried him back to the village. The incident deepened Benito's cynical dis-trust of his fellow men. Casting himself in the role of avenger, next day he sought out the deserters one by one and beat them mercilessly with a piece of oak firewood.

Dreams of power and glory first began to glimmer in his restless mind on cold winter evenings when he and his brother Arnaldo warmed themselves in front of the smithy fire, drinking wine with their father as he read aloud to them with relish from his favorite book, *The Prince*, by Machiavelli.

Signor Mussolini also aroused Benito's interest in ma-chinery by letting him help build a small threshing machine from parts he had collected and forged. Forever afterward Benito was fascinated by machines and engines of all kinds, and took great pride in his mechanical ability. Fixing things with his hands also satisfied his restless need for physical activity.

He could never bear to be still for any length of time. Once, bored with nothing to do, he spotted an old peasant hoeing laboriously on a farm about a mile away in the valley below Dovia. He suddenly sprinted off at top speed until he reached the old man. Snatching the hoe out of his hands, he finished the job as the peasant shrugged and sat down under a tree to smoke his pipe. Drenched with sweat, Benito returned the hoe in silence and trotted home contented.

When his mother had taught him all she could, Benito was sent to a school at Predappio, two miles away, a small hamlet of neat vineyards and shabby stone and stucco houses dominated by ruins of an ancient castle. Aware of his reputation as a tough guy, the boys of Predappio arranged a special reception for him on the first day. As he arrived, eleven boys lined up and hurled a barrage of stones.

Benito accepted the challenge and flung stones back at his tormentors with deadly accuracy until the school bell put an end to the war. Returning home in the evening for supper, he did not reach for the bread or *fromaggio* for fear his mother would see the gashes on his hands and weep that he had broken his promise to behave at the new school.

Each morning brought a fresh pitched battle. Benito grimly refused to retreat an inch, despite the odds against him. Bruised and bleeding, he exulted in playing the role of lone hero against the mob and enjoyed proving his courage. His adversaries at last offered him their hands in admiration, and not long afterward were following his lead in raids on vegetable patches and fruit orchards. He always insisted upon the lion's share of the spoils, and no one dared challenge that claim.

Sometimes he liked to steal away alone to the ruins of the old castle above Predappio which dated back to the time of the Caesars. His back against a crumbled wall, he would imagine the great palace as it had been at the height of Roman grandeur and muse how thrilling it must have been to live in those spectacular times. Someday, perhaps, a new Caesar would restore Italy to its ancient glories.

By the time he graduated from the Predappio school, his mother was at her wit's end about what could be done to tame her wild hellion before he got himself into serious trouble.

"He must go away to a boarding school, Alessandro," she told her husband anxiously. "Someplace he can meet a better class of children. Where the discipline is stricter." She caught her breath, then ventured, "The school at Faenza?"

"What?" roared her husband. "A school run by Salesiani priests? *Never*, woman! I'd be the laughingstock of the commune. Whoever heard of a Socialist letting his son's head be filled with church nonsense?" But shortly afterward, still grumbling, he hitched up the donkey cart and drove his older son to Faenza.

Benito's reception at the new school was again anything but cordial. Finding himself looked down upon by richer boys who received favored treatment, he provoked one fight after another.

"Mussolini," thundered the master friar, "your soul is black as hell. I warn you—confess your sins, repent before it's too late! I would have expelled you long before this, except for your poor mother's tears. But my patience is worn thin!"

Miserable and lonely, Benito tried to run away from Faenza, but was quickly overtaken and brought back. Ordered to beg forgiveness or face severe punishment, he refused and for almost two weeks had to kneel on grains of stale maize for four hours a day. On the tenth day, he could scarcely walk, but he kept grimly silent. When his punishment was over, he became more uncontrollable than ever. Flogged by an exasperated teacher, he screamed curses and hurled an inkwell at him, forfeiting both his recreation periods and meat at meals.

One day an older and stronger boy sneered at him and called him "the son of anarchist trash." Benito flew into battle. Finding himself outmatched physically, he drew a concealed knife and slashed the other boy's arm. This was the last straw for the long-suffering friars, and Benito was expelled at the end of his second year at Faenza.

"He has disgraced himself," his mother wept.

"No!" roared his father. "He is a true Mussolini—fighting for his honor against the priests and their jackals!"

Back home once more, Benito's education continued informally. He listened to violent political discussions his father enjoyed with workers who wore Garibaldi caps, black and red cravats and untrimmed beards. Interest in national affairs had been high since 1871, when Giuseppe Garibaldi, a fiery Italian revolutionist, had raised an army to free his countrymen and unite them in a single nation under the House of Savoy. But the new kingdom, instead of providing food and jobs for the hungry, had squandered its resources trying to carve out a colonial empire in Africa, in imitation of the great powers. Angry Italian workers found themselves as badly off under King Victor Emmanuel III as they had been before Italy's independence and seethed with discontent at what they considered a betrayal of Garibaldi's dream.

Benito grew more and more interested in the fierce debates at the local inn and at home over whether the ideas of Bakunin, Mazzini or Karl Marx offered the working class the best plan for winning control of Italy and turning it into a Socialist state.

He began to absorb the revolutionary traditions of the region he lived in—a land famous for harboring swashbuckling military adventurers known as *condottieri*. His father told him that when Garabaldi had been driven out of Rome in 1848 with a price on his head, he had fled to the Romagna. Here, despite threats of persecution and ruin to anyone who helped him, Garibaldi had found refuge. The whole region knew where he was, but not one voice betrayed him to Rome.

It did not escape Benito that some of the men who slept overnight in the Mussolini smithy were also being sought by the police for political violence. Unrest in the Romagna was growing rapidly, particularly among workers who were losing corn-threshing jobs to the new machines. In protest, the Socialists of Predappio were voted into office, and Alessandro Mussolini became mayor. He lost no time in organizing the first labor union in all of Italy.

One day, as Rosa Mussolini walked through the dingy hall of her home, she was startled to hear passionate shouting behind the closed door of the boys' room. Listening, she grew terrified as she realized that it was Benito's voice and he was alone. She beat on the door with her fist until he unlocked it.

"Benito, Benito," she faltered. "Have you lost your senses? All that shouting! Only madmen talk to themselves!"

He laughed, took her hands in his and kissed them.

"It's all right, Mama. I was simply practicing a little oratory, like Papa." He thrust his chin out confidently, and his black eyes shone with a strange brilliance she had never seen before. "Papa frightens only the landlords of little Predappio. But believe me, Mama, when I tell you—the time is coming when *all of Italy* will tremble before *me!*"

Social unrest, following widespread unemployment, continued to sweep through most of Europe during the 1890's and 1900's, and millions of Italians immigrated to South

America and the United States. Benito was fifteen when he turned out with the rest of Dovia and Predappio to wave a sad farewell to nine families leaving for Brazil. Tears of indignation glistened in his father's eyes as he watched old friends, bent low by the loads on their backs, disappear down the creaky platform steps, lit by flickering oil lamps, to the narrow railroad landing below.

"Take a good look, Benito," the blacksmith said bitterly. "See how our rulers reward those who slave for Italy. What did the workers' riots in Milan teach them? Only how to proclaim martial law! So now our neighbors have to leave their homes to save their babies from starving to death!"

His wife, weeping for friends she knew she would never see again, blew her nose. "One day we'll lose Benito like this, too, if you insist on making him a mechanic."

"But, Mama, I *love* to work with machinery."

"Your mother is right," his father growled. "There's no future in Italy anymore for hands. Only for wits! Learn how to manipulate people, not machines. Be a union organizer!"

"No," Rosa Mussolini said firmly. "Benito is going to be a teacher. Italy will never have enough teachers."

Benito decided to consult the one person in Dovia he knew had the power to predict the future. Old Giovanna, a village crone widely respected as a witch, was credited by rumor with three husbands, all of whom she was alleged to have done away with mysteriously. Taking a fancy to the handsome boy, she read his fortune in the entrails of a freshly killed chicken as the wind blew from the south.

"I see you in a beautiful palace," she croaked. "Greater than a king you are, because kings rush to do your bidding. The whole world shakes at the thunder of your voice. You have made all of Africa a slave colony for Italy. But you are surrounded by dangers, within and without." Her voice rose shrilly. "Listen to no one—only to the instincts of your own blood!"

Thrilled speechless, Benito seized the old crone's hand and kissed her gnarled fingers. After he had gone she chuckled to herself at the boy's credulity. But from then on he sought her company constantly, learning as much as he could about his own future. The sophistication of his later education never shook his belief in the occult powers of old Giovanna, and he always heeded her warning to trust his intuition over his logic.

At his mother's insistence that he study for a teacher's license, Benito attended the Instituto Magistrale in Forlimpopoli. Here his outthrust chin and aggressive manner provoked the usual clashes and knife fights. When he stabbed one opponent, the outraged master of the school expelled him, but then relented out of respect for the good name of Mayor Alessandro Mussolini and let Benito return as a day student boarding in town. Relieved at this narrow escape, Benito wisely decided to settle down to some hard study and soon demonstrated an intellectual brilliance that established him as the leading scholar of his class.

But the temptations of living by himself in town, away from all supervision, were scarcely to be resisted by a hot-blooded sixteen-year-old. He spent many evening in Forlimpopoli's cheap dance halls testing his magnetism on the local girls.

The seeds of revolutionary protest implanted in him by his father now began to flower. He led a student revolt to improve the quality of the bread served at the institute, after first stirring his schoolmates with inflammatory manifestos he wrote himself. Once he climbed a high hill near the school with a friend and startled his companion by musing out loud, "What a wonderful jumping-off spot for conquering the world!"

In 1901, he scored the highest final exam marks in the history of the Instituto Magistrale and graduated with a diploma that entitled him to teach elementary school. Returning home, he found no local teaching job open, so he applied for the post of town clerk in Predappio. He was turned down.

"The boy is scarcely eighteen," the new conservative mayor told the town board. "Besides, he's a dangerous Socialist like his father!"

When word of these remarks reached the ears of Alessandro Mussolini, the blacksmith rushed to Predappio in a towering rage. Confronting the mayor and town councilors, he brandished his fist furiously and shouted, "You will regret this, mark my words! The time will come when all Italy will laugh at Predappio for refusing to have Benito Mussolini as town clerk. And when that day arrives, you will be lucky if Predappio is not burned down around your ears for this insult!"

♦ 2 ♦
DOWN AND OUT IN SWITZERLAND

Mussolini finally won an appointment as a temporary teacher at a rural school in Gualteri on the banks of the Po. His wide-brimmed black hat and flowing black tie were soon a familiar sight each morning as he walked barefoot from his pension to the school, his shoes slung around his neck to keep them clean. Enjoying his first real taste of power, he ruled his classroom with an iron hand, in unconscious imitation of the harsh taskmasters he had hated as a schoolboy.

One day when a local orator failed to show up at the unveiling of a bust of Garibaldi in the market square, voices in the crowd milling impatiently in the hot sun cried, "The schoolteacher! Let Mussolini speak!" He was rushed to the table that served as a platform. Staring out at the sea of upturned faces, he felt a surging sense of excitement. For an hour and a half he spoke extemporaneously on Garibaldi as a revolutionary, with such stirring effect that the marketplace thundered with applause.

It was a great triumph for the teen-age orator, and might have led to political opportunity if he had not made some serious personal mistakes. Painfully conscious of his tender years, he had sought to seem older by dancing, drinking and playing cards with local young bucks in their twenties. He joined their raids on Sunday village dances, which they broke up by brawling and carrying girls off over their shoulders. Anxious to prove himself their equal as a dare-devil, he brandished chairs and traded kicks with a ferocity that earned the respect of his rowdy companions, but hardly endeared him to the solid citizens of Gualteri.

The outraged mayor, a bootmaker by trade, summoned the schoolteacher. "Mussolini," he fumed, "your behavior outside the classroom is a disgrace! From now on I order you to stop running around with that mob of hoodlums!"

Mussolini's black eyes glittered. "The beggar's pay I get to teach here," he snapped, "doesn't buy me body and soul! Let the bootmaker stick to his last!"

"Mussolini, you're fired!"

Shrugging, he returned to the pension and packed. Wrestling with his conscience briefly, he sat down and brazenly dashed off a telegram: "My sweetest darling mother, I have a debt of honor, and if you do not send me ten dollars instantly by telegram, I shall be forced to kill myself. God bless you, my adored mother, if you never again see me alive. Your Benito."

On his last morning in class he ordered his students to write an essay on a theme reflecting his own thoughts of the moment: "By Persevering You Arrive." "When you have a goal," he explained, "you must let nothing stand in the way of your achieving it. Pay any price you must for success, because an honorable failure is of no use to anyone!" When the noon bell sounded for the last time, he returned to his room to find that money had arrived from Predappio. He caught the next train for Switzerland.

"I did not want to go back to my family," he explained later. "It was too narrow a world for me, with affection to be sure, but restricted. In Predappio one could neither move nor think without feeling at the end of a short rope. I had become conscious of myself, sensitive to my future. I felt the urge to escape. Money I had not—merely a little. Courage was my asset. I decided to be an exile."

He felt the urge to broaden his horizons and satisfy the restlessness that at nineteen now drove him to keep constantly on the move. Growing unemployment and strikes in Italy also made him feel that he could find a job more quickly in Switzerland, especially since he was willing to do manual work. Teaching, he had discovered, didn't provide enough outlet for his immense physical energy.

Changing trains at Chiasso, he bought a paper and read it at the station while waiting for the Swiss express. A news item with a Predappio dateline caught his eye. The town had an election in which Socialists had clashed with Clericals, and one of the demonstrators sentenced to jail had been Alessandro Mussolini. Mother of Mercy, what was he to do? How could he continue on to Switzerland, leaving his father in prison, his mother torn by grief? But if he went back to Predappio, what could he possibly do to set his father free? The Lucerne express roared into the station as he wrestled with the dilemma. At the last moment, he decided to carry out his original plan, and swung aboard the train.

An unpleasant shock awaited him when he arrived in Switzerland. He quickly discovered that the tiny mountain republic was crowded with emigrés from Italy seeking jobs, most of them despised and ill-treated by the Swiss. Mussolini was no stranger to humiliation, but never before had he been scorned simply because he was Italian.

A temporary job in a chocolate factory finally turned up in Orbe, near the beautiful town of Lucerne. He next worked as a laborer, carting a wheelbarrow full of heavy stones up to the second floor of a building under construction. Though he was strong, he groaned under the strain of a backbreaking eleven-hour day that ended with swollen muscles that twitched convulsively. He was too exhausted to do more than roast some potatoes, then throw himself fully clothed on the pile of straw that served as his bed.

On the third day, as he staggered up a plank with his limbs giving beneath the weight of the stones, the contractor approached him with a sour expression. "Look alive, you!" he snarled. "Your clothes are too clean for a laborer doing an honest day's work!" Mussolini choked back his fury, but at the end of the week he quit and demanded his pay of thirty lire. The Swiss counted out twenty. "There's what I owe you," he said contemptuously. "And consider it stolen money!"

Recalling the incident later, Mussolini said, "What was I to do to him? Kill him? What did I do to him? Nothing. Why? Because I was hungry and had no shoes. I had worn a pair of light boots to pieces on the building stones which had lacerated both my hands and the soles of my feet. Almost barefooted, I simply took myself off to an Italian's shop and bought a pair of hobnailed shoes."

Deciding he had had enough of central Switzerland, he entrained west to Lausanne on Lake Geneva. Here his spirits brightened as he descended the charming hill city to Place St. François, enjoying the clean beauty of the houses, the flowers spilling over the balconies, the cordial policemen who saluted when he waved to them, the Alps half-hidden in clouds. In this paradise, surely, his luck was bound to change!

The money he had earned at Orbe lasted him a week as he trudged around Lausanne seeking employment, without success. Pockets empty, except for a Karl Marx medallion which he fingered for comfort as the devout fondle a cross, he wandered about hungry, unkempt, roofless. Late one afternoon gay strains of orchestra music led his steps to the quay, where he stared over the garden rail of the fashionable Hotel Beau Rivage at well-dressed tourists dining and dancing. Faint with hunger, he closed his eyes and listened to the soft rich laughter and rustle of silks and words in languages he did not understand. His despair slowly turned to blind hatred. He saw himself rushing into the hotel, snatching rings and necklaces, and choking any bourgeois who dared to object.

Seeking a place to spend the night protected from the cold winds blowing from the lake, he first tried a public lavatory, then the lee side of an old barge; finally he found a sheltered spot under the Great Bridge of Lausanne.

The days passed with agonizing slowness, each dawn bringing fresh despair to the disillusioned young vagabond, now gaunt, lean, hollow-cheeked, soiled and tattered. One day, he vowed grimly, one day. . . ! On one sunny autumn Thursday, lightheaded with hunger, he caught sight of two Englishwomen sitting on a bench eating bread, cheese and eggs. Unable to control himself, he snatched the lunch from one of the women, wolfing it voraciously. The ladies were too shocked or frightened to protest. "If they had," Mussolini admitted later, "I would probably have strangled them! I was so delirious from starvation."

He spent his nights sleeping under the Great Bridge, consoling himself that the fresh air was better than the filthy, evil-smelling lodging houses which were all low-paid laborers could afford. One night, however, the shivering youth sought shelter by crawling into an empty packing case. Discovered in the morning by police, he was sentenced to a day in jail as an undesirable vagrant. The magistrate strongly hinted that he could contribute to the loveliness of Lausanne by leaving it.

"Like father, like son," Benito brooded grimly. "The

jailbird Mussolinis!" But even as he clenched the bars of his cell, he determined that the son would *not* be like the father. Alessandro Mussolini was eternally doomed because he relied on his revolutionary tongue alone. The son would be a man of action, who used naked power to seize authority from his enemies, then turned it against them mercilessly. Freed in the morning, he left Lausanne with new iron in his soul, iron slowly tempered to steel during ten more arrests and imprisonments.

Out of work more often than not, miserably paid when he did find a job, he learned how to get by on the barest subsistence, waiting stoically for his fortune to change. He quickly learned the trick of never spending his last twenty-five cents. As long as he could produce a Swiss franc when stopped by a gendarme, he could not be deported from the republic of Switzerland as a vagabond. Even when faint with hunger, he kept one precious talisman unspent.

In whatever Swiss city he happened to be, Mussolini spent his evenings at the local Italian Socialist club made up of fellow emigrés. Switzerland had become the center of European discontent because of its tradition of asylum for victims of political persecution. Revolutionaries from Italy, Russia, Finland, Czechoslovakia and other countries met in the cafés to discuss Karl Marx and plot rebellion.

Returning to Lausanne, Mussolini fell in with a group of illiterate Socialist masons at the Café Boch and impressed them with his erudition and eloquence. They made him secretary-organizer of the Lausanne Association of Bricklayers and Manual Laborers, taught him how to cement window cornices and got him jobs. He proved so effective a spokesman that they gave him the honor of scrambling up to the parapet of every new building to fly the ceremonial flag of completion. He loved the dramatic moment when the wind, whipping the flag out of his hands, inspired a great cheer from workers below.

Now that he was leading men at last, Mussolini eagerly read book after book to learn all he could about the art of leadership. He was also deeply influenced by Professor Vilfredo Pareto, whose lectures he attended at the University of Lausanne. Pareto ridiculed the Marxist idea that historic events were the inevitable consequences of economic pressures; he insisted that history is simply a series of accidental occurrences brought about by unpredictable and often illogical human behavior. Nothing was certain except constant surprise, constant change. Successful leadership consisted simply of trimming sail swiftly to change course with each new shift of the wind. This credo became Mussolini's guiding principle in his pursuit of power. Each time he contradicted himself in speech or action, enemies denounced him as an opportunist, a turncoat, a hypocrite, an unstable eccentric, a liar. But in his own eyes he was only shrewdly following the teachings of Pareto.

Mussolini used his years of political apprenticeship in Switzerland to develop his talents as a soapbox orator and rabble-rouser. He loved to sway audiences with his eloquence, which he often directed against religion. One summer evening he stopped an Italian priest and in a loud voice offered to prove that God did not exist. As a crowd gathered, he borrowed a watch and announced, "I give God five minutes to strike me down and prove that He isn't a hoax. If I'm still alive after that time, ladies and gentlemen, I will let you draw your own conclusions!"

Once he went to a crowded hall to hear Emilio Vandervelde, the Belgian Socialist leader, speak on "Christ, the First Socialist." Mussolini listened impatiently, then mounted a chair and cried out to be heard.

"Why glorify a bungler like Jesus and His church?" he roared arrogantly. "He and his followers sabotaged the great Roman Empire. They killed the force and courage that made Rome great and Romans immortal! Even as a crusader, what was Christ but an insignificant little man who took two years to convert a few villages, and whose disciples were a dozen ignorant vagabonds, the scum of Palestine? Compare Christ's insignificant accomplishments to Buddha's forty volumes of doctrine and forty years of winning over half the world!"

The audience broke into appreciative applause. Hands on hips, Mussolini grinned cockily at his adversary, who replied dryly, "If Jesus was as ineffective as that young man suggests, I wonder how He and His dozen ignorant vagabonds were able to bring down the powerful Roman Empire in ruins. As for Christ's inability to match Buddha's forty years of teaching, I might remind my young friend that it was not entirely Jesus's fault that a certain misfortune due to His revolutionary preaching cut short His career!"

Mussolini flushed and the hall rocked with laughter.

During the long winter months in Switzerland when construction was impossible, he had to find other jobs to support himself. But work was scarce, and he went from canton to canton seeking menial employment. In Geneva he worked as an errand boy for a wine shop, pushing a little cart full of bottles. In June, 1903, shortly before his twentieth birthday, he organized a strike of Berne stone workers, urging them to use violence to win their demands. This was too much for canton authorities, who threw him into jail for twelve days, then expelled him from Berne. He went to Geneva, organized another violent strike, and was expelled again.

Suddenly word reached him that he was under sentence of a year's imprisonment in Italy for desertion because of his refusal to report back for military service. When he turned up in Zurich, international revolutionaries in the cafés now received him warmly as a genuine political refugee like themselves. Here he met Angelika Balabanoff, a middle-aged woman who was the recognized "soul and moving force" of Russian plotters in Switzerland, and whose co-conspirators against the Czar were Lenin and Trotsky. Tiny, hunchbacked, crack-voiced, she was a brilliant woman who spoke six languages and knew how to agitate skillfully in each one. Mussolini revered her, and for ten years she was his preceptor in the arts of revolution.

Anxious to imitate Angelika, he set out to learn languages and eventually taught himself some Russian, English, Spanish, German and French. Through her he met Lenin and Trotsky who, even in 1904, thirteen years before the Russian Revolution, were already its architects. One evening at a café, over bread, meat and bock beer, the three Russians discussed their young Italian friend in French as though he were not present.

"Mussolini's weakness is that he's a revolutionary only because he hates being poor himself, not out of genuine sympathy for the working class," Angelika said dryly. The daughter of a deceased rich Russian merchant, she had given away her entire inheritance to needy families. "And he's full of self-pity—"

"I have to be!" Mussolini cried. "I'm educated. I have abilities. Yet look at the rags I wear!"

"—too excitable, too neurotic, too unwashed, and he wastes his time in silly attacks on religion."

Trotsky chuckled, adjusting thick glasses on his wrinkled face. "Why do you bother with him, then?"

"He *does* have fire, eloquence and leadership ability."

Lenin nodded. "But he must stop dreaming of personal revenge for his humiliations. Teach him, Angelika, the importance of losing himself in the class struggle."

Mussolini listened thoughtfully, ate hungrily and said nothing. He was grateful to the Russians for their interest in him, eager to learn what they could teach him. He determined he would even find a way to bathe more often, if that would please Angelika Balabanoff!

Soon afterward he was eating in the same café with three Italian friends. When the waitress brought the bill, which totaled twenty cents more than he had expected to pay, he growled, "All right. I'll bring it tomorrow."

"Nein!" She shook her blonde curls. "You pay now!"

When he refused she summoned the proprietor, a thick-waisted Swiss with a brush mustache. He clamped a heavy hand on Mussolini's shoulder, which the young Italian, eyes flashing with fury, promptly swept away.

"They're treating me like a thief!" he roared to his friends. "Let's teach them how to behave to Italians!"

The next instant the café was a battleground, customers scrambling for cover as tables, beer glasses, chairs, bottles and hat racks went flying in all directions. When the Italians had finished, Mussolini grinned at the appalled proprietor and promised blandly, "I'll bring your twenty cents tomorrow."

When the police came rushing up, his three companions promptly fled, leaving him to struggle with the furious café owner. Sent to jail for ten days and then ordered out of Zurich, he decided to return to Berne, but there was one slight obstacle. His passport had expired, and to get a new one meant returning to Italy, where he faced arrest and a year in jail as a draft dodger. He altered the expiration date on his passport from 1903 to 1905. When this forgery was discovered, he was ordered deported, not just from Berne, but from all of Switzerland, to Chiasso on the Italian border.

"You cannot send me away like a mangy dog!" Mussolini protested bitterly. "Is Switzerland only a bogus democracy?"

As he was taken in handcuffs to the train, a Socialist deputy in the Grand Council of Geneva angrily denounced his government for violating the Swiss tradition of political asylum. The Minister of State meekly admitted that Mussolini should be allowed, at least, to choose his country of exile. Vastly relieved, the deportee decided to go to Trento, now in northern Italy, but then a part of the Austro-Hungarian Empire. Here a recommendation from Angelika Balabanoff won him a job with the Socialist paper *Avvenire*.

"Greatness may lie ahead of you," she wrote him, "if you will remember to use plenty of soap and water daily in your ears. Not only to show that an agitator can be clean, but also to let you hear the cries of the working class a little more distinctly!"

In 1905, King Victor Emmanuel III of Italy granted a general amnesty to all political refugees and draft dodgers abroad, provided the latter returned to Italy to serve their required term in the army. Mussolini hesitated, then decided to change direction again with this new twist of fortune. A bit sheepishly he wrote to Angelika, "There is a yearning for home which blossoms in the hearts of all Italians."

Rosa Mussolini almost fainted with joy when they were reunited. Mother and son wept unashamedly and even gruff Alessandro blinked rapidly to keep back the tears. Benito's brother Arnaldo and his sister Edvige, who had grown astonishingly plump, could scarcely tear themselves away from the family wanderer. For two months he stayed in Dovia, helping his mother teach school. Arnaldo told him quietly, "Mama has not been well. And no wonder! She kills herself with work and doesn't eat. You know Mama—food for the family, clothes for the family, money for the family, nothing for her!" Benito, remembering the outrageous letter he had written to frighten his mother into sending him the fare to Switzerland, and remittances he had received from her since, had the grace to feel ashamed.

He left home once more when he was called up to join the Tenth Bersaglieri Regiment, elite of the Italian infantry, who proudly wore green cock feathers in their hats and marched on the double to demonstrate their discipline and spirit. Their emphasis on gymnastics delighted Mussolini, who quickly established himself as the fastest runner and best high jumper in his company.

However, shortly after he joined the Bersaglieri, he received word that his mother was dangerously ill. Granted a furlough, he rushed home by the next train, in time to see his mother before she died.

For days he was inconsolable, silent. His father kept a copper vessel full of spiced wine brewing, and frequently refilled the glasses of his two sons as well as his own. Sometimes the three men dozed off as they sat in front of the kitchen fireplace, behind bolted windows and locked doors. When they awoke it was morning, the fire was dead, and the room was filled with the fragrance of wine that brought back memories of his mother.

• 3 •

"DOWN WITH WAR!"

Finishing his army service, Mussolini accepted a job teaching elementary grades at Caneva. Now sporting a fierce black mustache, he was something of a terror to his pupils, who were in awe of his tempestuous moods, the violent banging of his desk with his fist. Growing steadily more dissatisfied in his role of teacher, he spent his spare time roaming restlessly through the commune of Tolmezzo in search of ways to discharge his explosive energy. He drank heavily, declaimed poetry in the cemetery, made advances to pretty girls, sought fights, roved the streets singing and shouting after carousing all night. "A year of moral deterioration" was his own judgment of life in Tolmezzo at the age of twenty-three. Dissipation brought on a breakdown in his health, causing ulcerlike stomach pains which continued to harass him for the rest of his life.

The thunder of social change was now rumbling louder in the cities of Italy. The workers of Milan had called the nation's first general strike. When Mussolini visited his home district in the summer of 1908, he found farm workers seething with resentment over growing unemployment because of the use of threshing machines. He called a mass meeting of workers, inflaming them into attacking a farmhouse and trying to prevent a tenant farmer from moving a machine onto his threshing floor. Mussolini was arrested, tried for armed threats and sentenced to three months in prison.

"Political persecution!" raged the workers. The authorities, fearful that they were making Mussolini into a labor martyr, decided to set him free after only ten day in jail. They found him too absorbed in a book by Nietzsche to listen. "Don't interrupt me until I finish this chapter!" he snapped.

After his release he looked around for another cause to champion and soon found it in the high, officially fixed price of milk. Arousing a storm of protest over "the plot against the babies of the working class," he led a mob of furious men and women into the town hall and up two flights to the mayor's office, threatening to throw that official out the window unless he promised to lower milk prices at once. The perspiring mayor hastily gave his word, and the mob roared triumphant approval of its dynamic leader. Mussolini's eyes glowed with the thrill of power. There was no doubt about it—the Italian masses were just waiting to be led by a man of action who did not hesitate to use force for noble ends!

Soon after the death of his mother, his father left the smithy in Dovia to operate a rundown little hostelry called the Bersaglieri Inn near the railway station in Forli. Here Alessandro Mussolini took as his common-law wife a widow named Signora Guidi, who had three daughters. One was a pretty, buxom, sixteen-year-old blonde named Rachele who worked as a housemaid. She and Benito fell in love when he joined his father at the inn in the summer of 1908, helping in the bar when he wasn't studying and writing in the Forli town library. But Alessandro would not hear any talk of their marrying, and betrothed Rachele to a surveyor from Ravenna.

"Leave the girl alone," he told his son sharply. "You have no job and no money. All you have is your politics, which will bring suffering to you and to any woman who shares your life. Think of what your own mother went through because of me!"

But Benito Mussolini had also made up his mind and could be just as stubborn as his father. One night, returning from the local theatre with Rachele, he called her mother and his father into the kitchen and suddenly produced a revolver.

"There are six bullets in this gun," he said in a low, intense voice. "If you don't consent to our marriage, one is for Rachele, the other five are for me!"

The alarmed parents yielded. Kissing Rachele on the brow, Alesandro muttered, "Take care, child. Storms follow wherever my son goes!" Benito ignored both a civil and religious wedding ceremony, just as his father had, and swept his unofficial bride off for a brief honeymoon in San Martino.

Early in 1910 the Forli Socialist Federation made Benito Mussolini secretary at a beggarly pay of 120 lire a month. Members talked of doubling his salary; he refused to hear of a raise. The nobility of these sentiments was not fully appreciated by Rachele as she struggled to maintain their home in a sparsely furnished bedroom and kitchen without the barest necessities.

Supper generally consisted of cabbage or endives, and never satisfied their young appetites. When a daughter, Edda, was born to them in September, 1910, they skipped several meals so that the twenty-seven-year-old father could buy a rough wooden cradle.

At this period of his life Mussolini was a curious combina-

tion of idealist and opportunist. He genuinely believed that
the Socialist party had failed dismally to provide dynamic
leadership for the workers of Italy, and needed to be swept
clean of stagnation by a strong fresh wind like himself.
To win attention he founded, wrote, edited and sometimes
helped to print a four-page penny weekly, *Class War,* which
poured vitriolic scorn on Socialist leaders who insisted that
Italian workers had to be educated before revolution was
possible. "It is malicious irony to put a book into the hand
of one whose belly is empty," he wrote. "First the bread,
then the alphabet. Only people who eat their fill are able
to think!" He called for more action, less talk, and ridiculed
the idea that revolution had to wait for the uprising of a
whole people. Echoing what he had learned in Switzerland
from Angelika Balabanoff, Lenin and Trotsky, he insisted
that governments had to be overthrown by the swift violence
of a small, armed, determined band of revolutionaries. Only
after this minority took power, he argued, would the masses
rally in support.

The verbal thunder of *Class War* began to be heard
beyond the Romagna. Enthusiastic letters and telegrams
started pouring in, and a hundred miles away in Milan,
Claudio Treves, editor of *Avanti,* the leading Socialist daily,
soon found it necessary to argue against Mussolini in his
newspaper.

Mussolini was jubilant. "They're beginning to tremble," he
told Rachele. "The party bosses can't ignore me any longer!"

In September, 1911, the Giolitti government of Italy decided to annex the trading center of Tripoli in Libya, a
Turkish possession in North Africa, with the secret blessing
of England and France. Under a flimsy pretext, Giolitti sent
an ultimatum to Turkey. When the Ottoman Empire rejected it, Italian troops occupied and blockaded the Libyan

coast. This display of raw colonial aggression shocked Italy's
Socialists.

In Forli twelve thousand Italians jammed into the public
gardens to listen to Benito Mussolini. Many new faces were
in his audience, people brought there by Pietro Nenni, a
moderate Forli labor leader, whose disgust with Giolitti had
swung him into the Socialist camp.

"The invasion of Libya means only useless and stupid
bloodshed!" Mussolini cried out. "We throw away our
money and disturb the peace of Europe for nothing. What
is Libya? A barren, sandy desert—a *nothing!* What does the
government want to annex it for? Nobody knows. Not even
the government!"

The gardens shook with the crowd's indignant roar.
Knowing the mob was his, he played upon it as skillfully as
he evoked the tones he wanted out of his violin. "If our
stupid government refuses to recall our troops, then we must
make a people's revolution against it! *Conscripts!* Refuse to
report to barracks! Do not let yourselves be sent to Libya
to massacre natives! *Workers!* Go on strike so that what you
make cannot supply the military! *Citizens!* Do not come
tomorrow with your arms hanging loosely by your sides!
Come with weapons! *Comrades!* Down with war!"

For the next two days Forli was plunged into a state of
revolutionary turmoil. Factories were shut down, barricades
were erected, huge mobs surged violently through the city.
Mussolini directed operations, aided by Pietro Nenni. A
mob rushed the railroad station to prevent a troop train
from leaving. Telephone poles were cut down and thrown
across the tracks. Then the mob swarmed through the train,
forcing soldiers onto the platform. Many troops joined the
demonstrators. Mussolini led one group with pickaxes in
ripping up tram tracks and overturning streetcars. Nenni

took charge of cutting all telegraph wires leading out of the city. Whenever the Forli police attempted to hold back a mob, they were routed by stones, clubs and hand-to-hand combat. Cavalry troops rode to Forli to put down the insurrection. When they finally galloped into the city, sabers swinging, the rioting mobs broke ranks and fled in panic.

Appalled at the failure of his followers to stand and fight, Mussolini jumped up on a fountain and tried to rally them. *"Viva la Revoluzione!"* he bawled desperately at the top of his lungs. But by now the crowd had split into individuals, each man intent upon saving his own skin. As Mussolini watched helplessly, a cavalryman raced by the fountain and, with a stunning blow from the flat side of the saber, sent him flying off his perch. Lying dazed on the stones of the piazza, the salty blood on his lips became diffused with a taste of bitter disillusionment.

He staggered home to find Rachele shaking with terror in her anxiety about him. When she saw that he had been hurt, she uttered a little cry of fright and rushed to get a basin and water to wash his wounds.

"Cowards, all of them!" he muttered in disgust as she sponged his face with tender compassion. "This is a nation of cowards, Rachele. They won't fight!"

On October 14, along with Pietro Nenni, he was arrested for eight crimes involving the Forli uprising. Awaiting trial in his cell, Mussolini found himself no longer indifferent to imprisonment. Now he worried what would happen to Rachele and the baby if he had to go to jail for a long term. His father had been right. Revolutionaries had no business getting married, giving hostages to misfortune. Thinking of his father, his eyes misted over in sadness. Shortly before the excitement in Forli, Alessandro Mussolini had died at the age of fifty-seven. Three thousand comrades came from all over the Romagna to follow the coffin of one of Italy's pioneer Socialists. How many, his son mused, would one day follow his own?

At the trial Mussolini conducted his own defense, blandly disavowing personal responsibility for the riots. "The truth is that when fifteen thousand workmen assembled at Forli, the demonstration and strike burst out from the crowd *spontaneously!*"

The court sentenced both defendants to a year in prison.

"I refuse to rot in jail that long!" Mussolini fumed to his friend Gino Giommi. "Get Stoppato to appeal my case. He's a first-class criminal lawyer."

"Stoppato?" gasped Giommi, shocked. "What will the comrades say if you ask to be defended by a Catholic?"

"The devil with politics! I've had enough of being suffocated behind bars. *Eleven times,* my friend!"

He was finally persuaded to accept a Socialist lawyer, who won a reduction of his sentence to five months. When he was finally freed, Rachele begged him to promise that he would lead no more riots. He looked at her impatiently.

"Don't you understand, Rachele? Revolution isn't a matter of choice for me anymore. It's my destiny!"

Early in 1912 an attempt was made to assassinate King Victor Emmanuel III. Among those making formal calls at the Quirinal Palace to express relief at his escape was the prominent Socialist leader Leonida Bissolati. Mussolini made impassioned speeches against Bissolati's "betrayal of the proletariat," and won nomination to the Socialist Congress at Reggio Emilia in July. His first words slashed out like a whip at the delegates in the crowded auditorium.

"You, Bissolati, have tried to justify your act of homage to the King after the attempt made on his life by the

anarchist D'Alba. . . . Tell me, Bissolati, how many times
have you paid tribute to a bricklayer who falls from his
scaffolding? How many times have you paid tribute to a
carter who falls off his wagon? How many times have you
paid tribute to a miner injured by a cave-in? *What is the
attempt on the life of a king but an occupational accident?"*

The hall exploded with excitement. Never before in a
Socialist Congress had such a devastating personal attack been
made from the rostrum. When the commotion subsided,
Mussolini continued with merciless denunciations of each
Socialist leader in turn, sparing Claudio Treves, editor of
Avanti, least of all. He demanded immediate expulsion of
all Socialist leaders who were on record as favoring peaceful
revolution by ballot, and replacing them with Socialists
who were not afraid of street action. When he sat down to
thunderous applause, Bissolati, Treves and the others tried
to defend themselves but were booed and jeered. The Congress voted to expel Bissolati and three other party leaders
and to remove Treves as editor of *Avanti.* Mussolini had
scored a stunning triumph.

Nevertheless he was considered too young at twenty-nine
to replace Treves, until his cause was suddenly championed
by an old friend who turned up on the party directorate—
Angelika Balabanoff. She had left Switzerland to help the
revolution in the seething industrial North of Italy. She took
Mussolini to lunch and told him the job was his. Overjoyed,
he begged her to work with him as his assistant editor . . ."To
keep me from making blunders!"

"All right," she snapped. "But if I'm to work next to
you, you must wash more often. How many times do I have
to tell you? Soap and water, Mussolini, soap and water!"

For almost two years he kept Angelika's desk beside his
own, consulting her on every decision of importance. Some

Avanti journalists cynically felt that he was winning a reputation as a great editor by picking the old woman's brains, but his vigorous, slashing articles swiftly jumped the readership of *Avanti* from 40,000 to 100,000. The language he used was blunt, aggressive. "I find the villain of my situation," he said proudly, "and give him a quick stab between the fifth and sixth ribs."

In November, 1913, riots broke out in the South of Italy, where low wages and hunger had made agricultural workers in Rocca Gorga desperate. Troops rushed to the scene, dispersing the demonstration by artillery fire and killing some villagers.

Mussolini was outraged. His editorials on the Rocca Gorga massacre appeared day after day, relentlessly, stirring the conscience of the nation. The worried Giolitti government decided to arrest him and his staff, charging them with "provocation of soldiers to disobedience and insulting the army."

"I am not afraid of prison, gentlemen," Mussolini told the court. "As the Russians say, to become a complete man it takes four years in a public school, two in a university and two more in jail!" Even the jury laughed. Folding his arms, Mussolini sought each juryman's eyes in turn with his blazing gaze. "Acquit us," he demanded. "Not because we didn't commit the offense we're charged with, but because we *did*. And because we promise to commit it again! Anyhow, what good is a country where thirty-six million citizens are compelled to think alike? We Italians should die of utter boredom and imbecility if we were not allowed to cry 'No!' when a government says 'Yes!' "

The jury voted enthusiastically for acquittal.

Mussolini's prestige kept soaring as he whipped up working-class fury against all his enemies—monarchists, Republicans, priests, generals, right-wing Socialists, munition-makers and Masons. Then a priceless opportunity fell into his lap. An anarchist soldier, Augusto Masetti, shot and wounded a colonel named Stroppa during the latter's patriotic harangue of troops about to be shipped off to the Tripolitan War. Premier Giolitti feared that a public trial might provoke a political uproar because of rising antiwar sentiment, so on his orders Masetti was given a hasty medical examination, declared insane and shut up in an asylum.

When these facts leaked out, "Save Masetti" committees sprang up all over Italy. The Socialists quickly recognized the cause as a stirring injustice that could unite all prolabor, antiwar forces into a powerful front against the monarchy. Meeting in Ancona in April, 1914, the Socialist Congress voted to make Sunday, June 7, a day of national protest.

"If police try to break up our demonstrations," Mussolini cried out to the aroused delegates, "we will immediately call a general strike and paralyze the nation!"

On the fateful Sunday, early morning clashes with police in Ancona led to the killing of three workmen. The Socialists promptly declared a general strike which grew into the famous *Settimana Rossa,* or Red Week, of 1914. In Milan the center of the storm was Mussolini. Under his direction "Committees of Action" attacked army barracks, fought police, set fire to church doors, threw up street barricades, blew up munition dumps, seized wealthy farms. But by the end of the week government forces had put down the wild insurrection.

"The attempt at revolution—the Red Week—was not so much revolution as chaos," Mussolini admitted in *Avanti.* "The reason—no armed leaders!" Although he had failed to overthrow the Giolitti regime, the fame he won as "the

Lenin of Red Week" elected him to the City Council of Milan.

Europe was already a powder keg with sparks flying when a Serb nationalist shot and killed Archduke Francis Ferdinand, heir to the Austro-Hungarian throne, at Sarajevo on June 28, 1914. The continent swiftly divided into two enemy camps—on one side the Central Powers: Germany and Austria; on the other the Triple Entente Powers: England, France and Russia. The first guns began roaring in August.

The outbreak of World War I threw Italy into a state of confusion. On paper she was committed to what was known as the Triple Alliance, a thirty-two-year-old defense pact with Germany and the Austro-Hungarian Empire, but many Italians hated and distrusted their northern allies.

Speaking for the Socialists, Mussolini denounced both camps: "This is an imperialist power struggle fought with working-class blood. It can only lead us back to barbarism, to the age of clans and tribes!"

Pressured on all sides, Premier Giolitti desperately tried to sit on the fence. He proclaimed Italy neutral, explaining that the Triple Alliance obliged her to join allies only in a defensive war. Mussolini was jubilant but suspicious.

"The moment Italy shows any sign of breaking its neutrality to back up the Central Powers," he warned Giolitti in *Avanti*, "the Italian proletariat would have but one duty— we say it out clearly and distinctly—that of rising in rebellion!" In public speeches he insisted sternly, "Our neutrality must be *absolute*," and ended with the ringing cry, "Down with war!"

Early in September at a meeting in Paris, the French Council of Ministers decided to bribe Mussolini to desert the banner of neutralism and sway Italy into the trenches on the side of France. Through Fillipo Naldi, publisher of a small Bologna paper already on the French payroll, Mussolini was offered a first-class paper of his own. At first he was indignant at the French assumption that his honor was for sale. Then he began to reflect that publishing his own paper could very well make him the next premier of Italy. He could still champion Socialism, but his *own* brand of Socialism, with no party bosses to interfere. And hadn't Professor Pareto advised, "Always be ready to turn when the road turns?" So he agreed to swing *Avanti* over to the Allied cause.

Soon afterward, *Avanti* began to astonish its readers by speculating that Italy might have a stake in an Allied victory after all. If the Central Powers won, Austria might invade Italy to punish her for neutrality.

Angelika Balabanoff grew increasingly wrathful. "Mussolini, you're an idiot!" she stormed. "What is this trash you're writing? Why wasn't I consulted first?"

He turned on her with a savagery that stunned her. "*I* am the editor of *Avanti*—not you! If you don't have the brains to understand what I am saying, resign!" She did so promptly.

On October 10 he made his first open bid to sweep the Italian Socialist party into the war camp of the Allies. His front-page article, "From Absolute Neutrality to Relative Neutrality," predicted both the defeat of Germany and Austria and the Russian Revolution. "If war breeds a revolution, can we be against it?" he demanded craftily. "He who makes no difference between one war and another, who considers all wars alike, is just as foolish as he is pigheaded!" This betrayal of Socialist neutralism aroused a storm of protest among the faithful. Meeting in cafés they asked each other the cynical question: *"Chi paga?* Who is paying?" Mussolini always denied that he had sold himself to France, but years later he admitted, "I needed a daily paper, I hungered for one. . . . To me money has always been detestable. But what it may do is sometimes beautiful and sometimes noble."

Meanwhile a new accusation rang in his ears: *"Warmonger!"*

• 4 •

TASTE OF STEEL

Entering the People's Theatre, where thousands of excited Milan Socialists had gathered to decide whether he should be thrown out of the party as a traitor, Mussolini debated with himself how best to persuade them he had acted properly in "turning his coat." The meeting opened in bedlam. Speaker after speaker denounced him for defying the official Socialist party line—opposition to the war. One colleague accused, "If the Kaiser had offered you twice as much as the other side, you would have agreed to keep Italy out of the pockets of England and France!"

Mussolini stood mute at the rostrum through a storm of yells, hisses and shouts of "Traitor! Hireling! Judas!" He was visibly shaken by the vehemence of those who once had cheered him.

Then, his jaw outthrust in proud defiance, he shouted, "You are harder to talk to than the capitalists! If you insist that I am unworthy to be a Socialist—"

"Yes!" rolled across the hall like thunder.

"—I tell you you are wrong! I am and will remain a Socialist, no matter *what* you decide!" He pleaded with them to be realistic because the Central Powers were going to be crushed. If Italy joined the Allies now, her spoils of war would include Fiume, Dalmatia and Austrian territory up to the Brenner Pass. This baldly imperialistic appeal provoked such an outbreak of fury that Mussolini found it impossible to continue. He could only fling one final impassioned cry at his accusers: "You hate me because you still love me!"

When he sat down in a black rage, a sudden silence fell over those who heard his last words. In an illogical way his reproach had struck home; the rage of the Socialists against the idol who had betrayed them was closer to anguish than fury. They did not expel him, but neither did they give him the vote of confidence he demanded. He resigned from *Avanti*.

On November 13, 1914, a new daily newspaper appeared, *Il Popolo d'Italia*—The Italian Nation. The masthead describing it as the "Socialist Daily Press" was an invitation to party members to read it with a clear conscience. In his very first issue Mussolini wrote, "I fling to you my call, O youth, youth of Italy. . . . This call is but one word which I pronounce boldly today without reservation, one fearful but fascinating word—*war!*"

He said later, "My first article in the *Popolo d'Italia* turned a large part of public opinion toward the intervention of Italy in the war, side by side with France and England."

The paper's circulation soared swiftly. Powerful support came from the famous Italian poet-adventurer, Gabriele D'Annunzio. The Giolitti government finally tottered and fell, replaced by a prowar ministry that quickly struck a bargain with the British. If Italy joined the Allies, she would be rewarded by large slices of the Dalmatian coast, including the port of Fiume.

On May 24, 1915, Italy declared war on Austria-Hungary and attacked in the mountainous Dolomite region. Meeting stubborn resistance, Italian troops settled down to prolonged trench warfare. Mussolini promptly volunteered for the front, but had to wait until September to be called up with the

11th Bersaglieri, composed of men he had trained with ten years earlier.

He found army life in the high Alps hard and tedious. The troops froze in terrible storms, slipped around in trench mud, often went hungry. Reared in poverty and toughened by prison life, Mussolini endured these miseries stoically and even volunteered for night patrols in enemy territory. Twice grenades burst close enough to shower him with soil and rubble. Promoted to corporal, he was hospitalized at Cividale by typhoid. Rachele visited him there with a hesitant request. Their second child would soon be born. If anything happened to him, she would be unable to claim a widow's pension to take care of the children, because they were not legally married.

To her great relief he did not object. "The Socialists say I'm not a true radical any longer anyhow, so I might as well turn absolutely respectable!"

They were officially married in January, 1916.

He returned to his battalion in time to join an advance to the snow-smothered summit of Mount Nero, where they dug into huge drifts only a few dozen yards from enemy trenches. The war was being fought blindly in Alpine clouds, both sides attacking and counterattacking in a savage seesaw. In the first few months of war on the Austro-Italian border, Italian casualties were 50,000 dead, 180,000 wounded. In a typical diary entry Mussolini wrote, "After a cannonade of twelve hours a great white silence has sunk over us—the snow. We are all buried. The storms at least blot out the dead hanging crucified on the barbed wire entanglements."

In May his regiment was relieved, and after a brief rest, they were sent to another war-churned battleground on the Carso, a rocky valley near Lake Doberdo. "Anyone who lives long on the lake shore," Mussolini reported grimly to *Il*

Popolo, "forgets forever how to smile." The morning wind
bore the stench of unburied corpses. The spring sky was full
of whistling shells. The water of the lake was unusable
because of a cholera outbreak, and for a whole month Mussolini never washed his face. He grew morbid under the
constant bombardment. "Dead and more dead," he wrote
Rachele gloomily. "What seas of blood have been drunk up
by the red soil of the Carso!"

Often both sides had a tacit understanding to fight a "live-
and-let-live" war, with firing restricted to scheduled times,
so that fewer men on both sides would die and each army
could have time out to rest, eat, delouse themselves and
smoke. Mussolini, however, had nothing but contempt for
such practical accommodations. During a lull one night he
spotted a match struck in the enemy lines. Seizing a hand
grenade he pulled the pin, held it until the last moment,
then hurled it at the target. There was a loud booming
crack and a flash of flame. A captain making his rounds
approached him, shaking his head reproachfully.

"Why did you do that, my son? Those soldiers you just
killed were sitting peacefully, doing us no harm. They were
probably smoking their pipes and talking of their wives
and children. Was it necessary to be so heartless?"

"Perhaps you would have liked it better," he said in-
solently, "if I had asked them to a Milan café with us?"

The captain stared at him for a moment. "I pity you if you
think that makes less sense than what you just did!"

A patrol reporting back at dawn revealed that Mussolini's
grenade had killed two Austrians and wounded five others.
The enemy, outraged by this breach of understanding between the lines, retaliated with surprise attacks. The front
quickly erupted into total war around the clock. Both sides
went sleepless as cannon fire agitated the earth beneath

their feet, and the explosions shook the walls of their trenches.

November, 1916, brought the onslaught of a dreadful winter. Thick, heavy rains that had buried the troops in mud and soaked them to the skin gave way to relentless snows. Condemned to immobility by the onslaught of rifle and machine-gun fire against anything that moved, the soldiers were frozen to the bone. Many complained of not being able to feel their feet.

Mussolini's Christmas present arrived two days late; on December 27 Rachele gave birth to their second son—a boy named Vittorio for the hope of victory. Having refused leaves many times, he finally accepted a furlough to see his son. When he found out how little Rachele and the children were given to live on by the government, he was furious.

Storming into the offices of *Il Popolo,* he wrote slashing articles demanding decent rations for soldiers' families and total support on the home front. "We who take on our shoulders the fatigue of the trenches and the deadly risks of battle," he thundered, "have a right to expect security in our rear!"

Shortly after returning to the front, he was transferred to a mortar battery. On February 22, 1917, he was in charge of trial-firing a trench mortar which became over-heated. When the mortar fired again there was a violent explosion. Five of the crew were killed instantly, and a great many more in the trench were wounded. Mussolini was hit by a shower of steel splinters and was hurled half-naked several yards away in a shower of dirt and smoke. He had been wounded in no less than forty-four places, the most serious being in the left thigh where a shell fragment had shattered the bone and driven dirty pieces of cloth into the wound. He was rushed to the hospital a few miles behind the lines, and the doctors agreed that he could not last out the night. Semiconscious, he overheard and understood.

"No!" he gasped in delirium. "I *refuse* to die! Even if all the doctors explode with exasperation! I snap my fingers at medical science. It is my destiny to live!"

He endured twenty-seven operations during which anesthetics, in short supply at the front, were used only twice. Continuous shelling forced the hospital authorities to evacuate most of the patients from the wards, but Mussolini's delicate condition did not allow him to be moved. He was cheered by hundreds of telegrams and letters pouring in from all over Italy and immensely flattered when the King himself asked to see him during a tour of the front.

"I'm proud," he wrote back to *Il Popolo,* "to have reddened the road to Trieste with my own blood in fulfillment of my perilous but patriotic duty." As soon as he was able to limp out of the hospital, he began writing furious editorials against the Socialists, who had told the Italian Parliament: "We will desert the trenches before the winter comes!" Mussolini was grimly aware that soldiers on leave were returning to battle in a sullen, antiwar frame of mind. The Russian Revolution of March, 1917, had set an example which the Italian Socialist party was urging as a model for Italy.

In October a combined Austro-German attack smashed through Italian lines at Caporetto, bottled up the Italian Third Army and threatened to swallow the whole northeast of the nation. Italian troops fled in disorder, and Germany announced the collapse of Italy.

Demonstrations for peace began to break out in Italian cities, led jointly by Socialists and Communists. The cry for peace became almost irresistible by December, when the Russians signed a separate peace with the Central Powers and ordered their troops home.

Enraged, Mussolini used the front pages of *Il Popolo* to roar "Stop!" at troops retreating from the front and at workers demonstrating in the cities. His left arm still semiparalyzed by a bomb fragment, he used his right hand to write passionate appeals for faith in the Italian Army. "Caporetto was only a moment of weakness and shame," he pleaded. "Such moments happen to all armies and all peoples in all periods of history."

His persistent eloquence was influential in rallying public opinion behind a renewal of the war effort. The government lowered the age for volunteers, and thousands of seventeen-year-old boys rushed to get into uniform. They were sped to the front with fresh Allied divisions. After fierce battles at the Piave River, the Austro-German advance was finally stopped.

Now the tides of war reversed. In four months the Austrian Army was routed and crushed, and on November 11, 1918, the war was over.

Wild scenes of victory in every Italian city were soon followed by a sobering tally of the cost. Over 650,000 Italians had been killed, 450,000 had been crippled and 100,000 had been wounded. Dismay grew deeper as soldiers returned home to find the economy in bad shape, with no jobs or bonuses.

Quickly sensing that the discontent of the veterans would soon shake Italy to its foundations, Mussolini set about winning more followers to his own cause. In Bologna, haranguing a crowd of returned soldiers, he cried out, "We have fought for the nation's future, and so that future is rightfully ours!"

A dozen different ideologies were now bidding for the

favor of the Italian people. Lenin was offering a new road
to the future with Communism. United States President
Wilson urged faith in the League of Nations and international cooperation. Don Sturzo, a priest heading the Catholic
party, was asking Italians to choose the path of "Christian
democracy."

"The masses are ready for a brand-new force," Benito
mused aloud to his brother Arnaldo, who was now assistant
editor and publisher of *Il Popolo*. "I can win them if I
can seize their imaginations with a new idea. *Any* idea—as
long as it stirs them emotionally!" He was becoming cynically confident that he could be all things to all men simply
by using only eloquent, glittering generalities, allowing
each man to interpret them to suit himself. "Nothing's easier
than to get a crowd roaring—*especially* when they don't
know what they're roaring about! I'll prove it to you,
Arnaldo. I'll be a candidate in the next Milan elections.
And I'll win on the sheer excitement in my voice!"

On February 18, four months after the Armistice, ten
thousand men, women and children surged through the
streets of Milan shouting, "Down with the militarists! Long
live the workers of the world!" Benito Mussolini watched
the three-hour demonstration from a window in the *Il Popolo*
building. In an editorial addressed to Italy's war dead, he
asked bitterly, "Do they want to forget the earth that was
soaked with your blood and to spit on your sacrifices? We
shall defend you even if we must put dugouts in the public
squares and trenches in the streets!"

When Arnaldo came in with papers his brother had to
sign to become a candidate in Milan's next elections, Benito
snapped, "I am not going to be a candidate!"

Arnaldo looked bewildered. "But yesterday you said—"

"Don't shackle me with words I spoke yesterday!" He

flung his arm toward the window. "Would you have me stand in the marketplace and show my military scars to *that* rabble?"

Political unrest swept rapidly through Italy, fanned by the government's inability to cope with unemployment, soaring prices, strikes and plant seizures. Prime Minister Nitti was also bitterly attacked for giving up Italy's postwar claims of territory in peace talks with the Allies. The fiercest denunciation came from Benito Mussolini and Gabriele D'Annunzio, Italy's celebrated poet-adventurer and war hero.

On March 23, Mussolini called a charter meeting of the "Milan Fighters' Fascio" in a room provided by the Merchants' Association at their clubhouse on Piazza San Sepolero. Among the fifty-four founders of Fascism attending that night were Bianchi, an embezzler; Tancredi, kicked out of the Anarchist movement for theft; Filippini, a lawyer disbarred for swindling; and Balbo, a former general who organized street assaults on Socialists. Also present were property owners frightened about Communism, and ex-*Arditi*, the Italian shock troops who had led attacks with daggers between their teeth and a grenade in each hand.

"Distinguished friends and comrades," Mussolini welcomed them, "your presence here tonight proves your awareness of our nation's dire peril. I see this little band of patriots as Italy's future 'supermen,' to borrow Nietzche's term."

He reminded them of the *fasces,* or bundle of sticks, carried by the Roman lictors of Caesar's day as symbols of authority. "By uniting our forces behind one powerful will, we can combine in the same unbreakable force!" They would be known as the *Fasci Italiani di Combattimento*— Association of Italian Fighters. Their flag would be the banner of the Arditi, a white skull insignia on a black background, and their uniform the black shirt of Romagna workers, plus a black fez.

All present rose and swore solemn allegiance to the Fascio and to Benito Mussolini as its leader. Cesare Rossi, a former Syndicalist, was elected secretary. Rossi later revealed that Mussolini picked an executive committee from the most enthusiastic applauders. Among them were two criminals with police records.

Beginning to taste the heady wine of power, Mussolini confessed to Margherita Sarfatti, a journalist on the staff of *Il Popolo,* "I'm obsessed with a wild desire that consumes my whole being. I want to make a mark on my era with my will, like a lion with a claw—a mark like this!" And his clawed fingers violently ripped the back of a chair cover.

There was national indignation when the Versailles Conference came to an end with a final denial of Italy's claim to Fiume and Dalmatia despite the heavy Italian population of both these areas. D'Annunzio furiously denounced Wilson as a "horse-cheeked false prophet . . . the greatest humbug earth has ever carried on its back!" Mussolini thundered daily at the "insanity of Versailles." D'Annunzio wrote him enthusiastically that together they would correct the mistakes of history.

The Socialists still had not forgiven Mussolini for selling out to the war camp. *Avanti* infuriated him by persistent references to "Mussolini, Judas of the working class" and "Signor Thirty-Pieces-of-Silver." His opportunity for revenge came on April 15 when 30,000 workers responded to the Socialists' call for an antigovernment parade through the streets of Milan. Mussolini swiftly dispatched a small but heavily armed band of Fascists. The two forces met on the Piazza del Duomo in unequal warfare—the workers threw stones, the Fascists used their revolvers, cudgels and daggers. The workers broke ranks and fled, leaving their dead behind in the street. Mussolini's men raced briefly in pursuit, then changed direction toward the premises of *Avanti*. Breaking in, they smashed the presses, destroyed the furniture and set fire to the plant.

In September D'Annunzio, at the head of a small band of armed Arditi, marched on Fiume and captured the port city without a shot being fired. A wave of jubilation and popular support for him swept over the Italian people. Mussolini lost no time in scrambling on the bandwagon. Calling in American reporters, he told them sonorously, "We are all agreed over Fiume. Fiume is entirely Italian, in language and in population." He urged them to appeal to Italian-Americans in the United States for funds "to feed the starving babies of Fiume."

In *Il Popolo* he also appealed for funds, and hurled his first challenge at the Nitti government. "The real government of Italy is not in Rome, but in Fiume! It is *that* government which we must obey!"

He decided the time was ripe to try for a seat in the Chamber of Deputies. In the November national elections one of the rival candidates he ran against was the famous musical conductor Arturo Toscanini. The campaign was one of the stormiest in Italian history. Mussolini's Arditi supporters made the offices of *Il Popolo* an arsenal of guns and bombs. Even the stove concealed bombs; one cold morning an office boy who didn't know it almost blew them all to pieces by trying to light a fire before he was noticed and quickly dragged away. The Arditi put on torchlight parades, singing war songs, firing pistols and Verey lights in the air. Bombs were tossed into Socialist meetings. Some Anarchist

candidates were seized, beaten up, forced to swallow huge
doses of castor oil poured down their throats through a
funnel.

When the Archbishop of Milan protested against the out-
rages of the Fascists, Mussolini himself stopped a man on
the street and gave him ten lire to deliver a package to his
critic. The package contained a time bomb which failed
to go off, fortunately for the Archbishop, who shortly afterward became Pope Pius XI.

After the ballots were counted on November 20, Mussolini
was found to have gone down to ignominious defeat,
garnering only 4,000 votes against a Socialist total of 200,000.
The staggering success of the Socialists gave them 150 seats
out of some 900 in the Italian Parliament. Jubilant victors
in Milan promptly organized a midnight torchlight parade.
Under a banner reading "Recovered from the Sewer," they
marched past Mussolini's home with coffins bearing the
symbolic political corpses of Mussolini and D'Annunzio.

In the morning police raided *Il Popolo* and found the
hidden caches of guns and bombs. Mussolini was arrested
for "armed plotting against the security of the state."
Arnaldo promptly headlined the next issue of *Il Popolo*:
MUSSOLINI, GUILTY OF SAVING ITALY AFTER
CAPORETTO, THROWN INTO PRISON!

His stay in San Vittore prison was brief. Toscanini and
a senator named Albertini persuaded Premier Nitti it would
be a mistake to make a martyr out of Mussolini, and he
was freed. But his stock soon sank even lower. Two assistant
editors on *Il Popolo* suddenly resigned, charging Mussolini
with having diverted contributions he had collected for the
children of Fiume to finance his election campaign.

One day he stopped in at the Milan post office to pick

up money-order contributions for Fiume from America. The clerks pretended not to know him. "Benito Mussolini—who's that?" they asked one another in mock gravity, enjoying his rising fury.

"You'll find out, you miserable Reds!" he raged, shaking his fist at them. "I'll have my revenge on the lot of you—in less than two years! Just wait!"

· 5 ·

MARCH ON ROME

To release the angry tensions that made him perpetually restless, he began daily fencing lessons in the courtyard of *Il Popolo* and took flying lessons at Bresso Airport from a war ace named Redalli.

One day while soloing he attempted a stunt landing to impress Redalli, and crashed. With characteristic bravado he limped away from the accident. No bones were broken, but the doctor ordered him to bed for several weeks. He went back to work in twenty-four hours. "I *will* myself to be well," he explained imperiously.

Like most countries after World War I, Italy was swept by postwar unrest arising from economic problems. The Socialists were winning tremendous popular support by attacking profiteers who had sent the cost of living soaring. The lira was now worth only 25 per cent of its prewar value. When the King entered the Chamber of Deputies to open the new session, Socialist members greeted him by singing *The Red Flag*. One strike followed another.

Mussolini began his second bid for power in 1920 by promising each angry group of Italians what they wanted to hear. He pledged to fight for bonuses for veterans, jobs for the jobless, land for tenant farmers, suppression of Bolshevism for frightened landowners and industrialists. Even his enemies acknowledged his hypnotic powers as a speaker.

"He carried away his audiences," admitted Bruno Buozzi, Secretary-General of the Federation of Italian Metal Workers. "He had a marvelous mobility in his face; he rolled his black eyes; his shoulders were agitated energetically; he modulated his voice; made long pauses; then suddenly burst out in the loudest tones, sweeping the crowd with him." Giolitti, once more premier, replacing Nitti, said dryly, "The ladies rave about him. There's no doubt about it—if Mussolini wanted to, he could become the greatest actor in the world!"

Still, by August Socialist influence prevailed to such an extent that workers had seized factories in ten cities in northern Italy, and in Sicily landless peasants had seized the farms of wealthy landowners. Premier Giolitti, fearing total revolution, simply sat tight and scoffed, "Let the workers and farmers see for themselves how hard it is to run a business successfully!" Then the railroad unions struck, and now Italian trains were not just late but totally stalled. Giolitti sent an emissary to *Il Popolo* to offer a secret bargain. If Mussolini would break with D'Annunzio, the government would put pressure on its *carabinieri* to join the Fascists, and also close its eyes to any antilabor violence by the Arditi.

"What a wily, hypocritical old fox!" exploded Arnaldo.

"No!" smiled Benito. "What a great patriot!"

His forces expanded rapidly to 30,000 *Fascisti*. When D'Annunzio sent pleas for troop support, money and food, Mussolini found himself "too busy" to reply. D'Annunzio begged him to visit Fiume; Mussolini swore he would, but failed to show up. Then Giolitti blockaded Fiume and threatened its destruction until D'Annunzio glumly surrendered.

"Let no one reproach me because I have not made that

little, easy, cheerful, pleasant thing called a revolution," Mussolini blustered in *Il Popolo*. "The Fascisti have never promised to make a revolution in Italy in the event of Fiume being attacked. I personally have never written to D'Annunzio to make him believe it. I do not bluff or talk hot air!"

On October 9, at a Fascist meeting in Florence, Mussolini began spelling out his own program for a "new Italy," which he now saw as a state run in the form of a big corporation with farmers and workers organized in government-controlled syndicates. And for the first time he openly revealed the contempt in which he held the average Italian.

"I do not tell you, O people, that you are as gods," he shouted. "As I love you truly, so I should say to you that you are dirty. You must arise and cleanse yourselves! You are ignorant. Therefore be willing to learn!"

Enjoying the secret support of Giolitti, he felt confident enough to drop *Il Popolo's* hypocritical subtitle, "The Socialist Daily" for a new image: "Journal of the Fighters and Producers." Now he began to attack both Socialism and Communism as systems of state ownership doomed to failure.

Through the winter of 1920–1921, undeclared civil war raged in the cities of Italy as Fascist squads attacked three hundred Socialist strongholds, killing over two hundred workers and wounding a thousand. During every battle, police and *carabinieri* were peculiarly absent, arriving only after the Fascists had fled, in time to arrest stunned and wounded workers. Victimized along with the Socialists were Social Democrats, Catholics and Anarchists. Outraged Socialist members of Parliament demanded that the Giolitti government take immediate action against the Fascists. "We will certainly look into the matter," Giolitti promised blandly. Reading this news item, Mussolini laughed.

The left-wing movement in Italy began to crumble under the hammer blows of Fascism. Giolitti received congratulations from the King for his cleverness in using the right to destroy the threat on the left. Meanwhile the Fascists were winning new support from workers who had lost faith in their leaders, from tenant farmers who hoped for land, from landowners who saw Mussolini as their savior against the frightening specter of Bolshevism. As the elections of May, 1921, approached, it was apparent to all that Benito Mussolini was once more a growing power in Italy.

He entered the elections at the head of a slate of thirty-four Blackshirts. Now he dared to spell out the real aims he had nurtured since his boyhood daydreams in the ruined castle of Predappio. Addressing huge crowds in Milan's Cathedral Square, he shouted, "In this age, instead of the reign of the masses, there must come the reign of one great leader! Only one man's brain, one man's will, can get the most out of the Italian people!"

He was challenged by his old enemy, Father Don Sturzo, who had made the Catholic party the strongest force in Parliament. "Mussolini is a brilliant extemporizer," Sturzo said dryly, "with the ability to seize every opportunity and profit by circumstances. It must be wonderful not to have to feel ashamed or apologetic for changing a dozen horses in mid-stream!"

Stung, Mussolini warned grimly, "Sturzo's nose is big enough to smell out heresy, and he is right to fear the heresy of Fascism, which will smash his ignorant church!"

As the elections drew near, Nikolai Lenin told a deputation of Italian Socialists visiting Moscow, "It's a pity you had to lose Mussolini. He is the one strong man who would have led you to victory!"

The May elections resulted in a stunning victory for

Mussolini. All thirty-four Fascists were elected to the Chamber of Deputies, and they wrested control of Milan, Bologna and Ferrara from the Socialists. Their leader had fulfilled his threat to rise from ignominious defeat to victory in less than two years and had increased his following from 4,000 to 178,000.

Mussolini told his brother with a chuckle, "Now that old fox Giolitti thinks he has me where he wants me. He hopes he can keep Fascism a tame and respectable pet in Parliament. But I've got a little surprise for him!"

"What kind of a surprise?"

"Arnaldo, what would you say if I told you I intend to sign a truce to cooperate with the Socialists and the Catholic party and end all violence between us?"

His brother blinked in astonishment. "You're joking!"

"If our three parties combined, we would have a vote of two hundred forty-nine in Parliament. Giolitti's Democrats have only a hundred and ninety-five. Now do you understand?"

In August, this truce was actually signed. Giolitti was stunned; no less so were members of the Socialist and Catholic parties. Most dismayed of all were Mussolini's Fascist followers, to whom the new alliance came as a total surprise. Rising shouts of protest were heard in the Blackshirt camp.

Mussolini cracked the whip of his authority in *Il Popolo*. "Remember the proverb," he warned, " 'Whoever does not employ the rod hates his son.' Everyone knows that Fascism is my son. I swear with the rods of my oath, my courage, my passion, I will either correct him or make his life impossible!"

But one Fascist group after another angrily refused to respect the truce. In September the Blackshirts of the Po Valley staged unauthorized attacks against Socialist cooperatives, Catholic clubs and labor unions, resulting in seven dead, twenty wounded. In Bologna they sang anti-Mussolini songs and posted signs: "Who has betrayed once will betray again!"

To stop the revolt in his ranks, Mussolini called a Fascist Congress in Rome in November. "You do not understand, you do not wish to understand, that the country wishes to work without being disturbed!" he shouted at his disgruntled followers. "I would enter an alliance with the devil himself to give our poor country five years of tranquility!"

"You must follow Fascism, not make up your own rules!" a Blackshirt shouted. "You must support local Fascists wherever they fight—not toady to Socialists and Catholics!"

Mussolini drew himself up imperiously. "I am busy with the affairs of Italy and Europe and the world—and you expect me to throw myself into your little local squabbles! No! I am *Il Duce,* the leader!" But the Fascist Congress rebuked him by voting against him. Mussolini replied with a thunderbolt. "I am a leader who leads, not a leader who follows! I resign!"

If the Fascists were bewildered and lost without their leader, their leader was even more lost without his power.

"I let pride trap me into a blunder," he told Arnaldo gloomily. "I built Fascism from nothing. It was my own creature, and I should never have let it slip its collar!"

Two weeks after his resignation he made a brazen about-face, taking the floor in Parliament to announce without warning that the peace treaty was dead and buried. "Italy's destiny," he thundered, "demands a holy crusade of Fascist violence against the oppressions of the Italian people by Socialists, Catholics and Democrats!" Delighted Fascist members, who had been ignoring him coldly, now cheered and embraced him. Arnaldo, editing *Il Popolo* in his absence,

obediently ran bold headlines: DOWN WITH PARLIA-
MENT! LONG LIVE DICTATORSHIP!

Mussolini met privately in Rome with Vecchi, Arditi
leader of the Fascists, to arrange for his restoration as head
of the party, but he was shocked to discover that real control
of the party had already slipped out of his hands. The Blackshirt organization was now being financed and controlled by
Italy's national association of industrialists and manufacturers.

"They are willing to have you back as Il Duce," Vecchi
told him, "provided you agree to carry out one order. They
want the Italian labor movement destroyed, and quickly."

"But of course," Mussolini replied smoothly. "How can
there ever be industrial peace until all workers are under
government control—and all government under a Duce?
I accept!"

The monster he had created was now his master.

In January, 1922, Mussolini attended a conference of
world diplomats at Cannes, France, to discuss injustices of
the Versailles Treaty. Returning to Milan, he found a new
challenge to his power. Italo Balbo, an arrogant, former
general who reveled in bloody street fighting, had organized
a new action junta called the "Quadrumvirate," which included De Bono, commander of the Blackshirt squads;
Vecchi, leader of the Arditi; Bianchi, now party secretary.

"We've had enough talk," Balbo told Mussolini bluntly.
"We want revolution and we want it now. Otherwise we'll
start a march on Rome without you!"

"Don't be a fool!" Il Duce growled. "Move too fast and
the government will join forces with the Socialists and the
Communists to crush us. Destroy the left wing first!"

But as soon as Mussolini left Milan for Parliament in

spring, Balbo ordered Dino Grandi, leader of the Blackshirts in Bologna, to seize the city for Fascism. Mussolini was furious. He wired Grandi to get out of Bologna immediately and ordered Balbo to make no further move without authorization. "Either obey the Duce," he threatened, "or I will call a Fascist Congress to have the four of you thrown out of the party as fools and traitors!"

His bluff worked, but nervous tension caused his stomach ulcers to flare up, and he had to live for days on nothing but milk. His temper grew short, not only with hotheaded Fascist extremists but also with Socialist deputies. He fought sword duels with ten different opponents, honor being satisfied by first blood drawn. His closest call from enemy steel, however, came one day when he entered a barber shop for a shave. The barber, who didn't recognize him, loudly proclaimed anti-Fascist views. Running his razor along Mussolini's throat, he sighed, "Isn't there any Italian with courage enough to assassinate that traitor Mussolini?"

In August, Socialists and other groups of the left called a general strike to protest the government's unwillingness to stop violence by Blackshirt squads. One ministry after another fell in a vain attempt to find a solution which would satisfy both right and left and restore peace to the nation. In desperation the King sent a secret message to Mussolini. Would he disband Fascism's action squads in exchange for a cabinet post in a "government of national union"?

Mussolini eagerly accepted, but Giacomo Matteotti, a popular Socialist deputy, demanded indignantly, "How can a man who hates popular government serve it?" Vigorous objections also came from Claudio Treves and from Don Sturzo. The King dropped the plan.

Before a Fascist Congress of 40,000 delegates in Naples Il Duce finally thundered an open Blackshirt challenge to the government. "We represent the spirit of Imperial Rome!" he shouted belligerently. "We scorn the foolish reverence for ignorant masses!"

He issued a proclamation of revolution, signed by the Quadrumvirate, and published it in *Il Po'polo.* "Either the government must be handed over to us," he warned, "or we shall seize it by marching on Rome!" Seated on a horse in the vast Piazza del Plebiscito, he raised his arm in stern salute to the thousands of Blackshirts who marched past him with blaring trumpets and snapping flags, roaring, *"Duce! A Roma! A Roma!"*

Now the King and the new Premier, Luigi Facta, were really shaken. They knew that this was no longer just Fascist oratory, but genuine insurrection. In desperation Facta hurriedly scheduled a Rome rally of Old Comrades, a powerful non-Fascist veterans' organization, and sped a request to Lake Garda for the presence of the one man who could make Mussolini hesitate to attack.

"I accept happily," wrote Gabriele D'Annunzio, "lifted to the pinnacle of joy at the thought of being with all my old comrades once more. A mysterious force compels me to Rome!"

But Mussolini, alerted by a Fascist network of spies in the government, promptly arranged another mysterious force that compelled the famous war hero to stay out of Rome. Unidentified assailants pushed D'Annunzio out of a fifteen-foot high balcony window, and he suffered severe head and neck injuries that addled his brain. Il Duce sent a note of deep sympathy.

On October 27, 1922, Mussolini gave the signal for three huge columns of Blackshirts to converge on Rome from different directions. There was no opposition from police or troops, and the Italian people simply barricaded themselves in their homes, watching the great drama in astonishment.

As the King received reports on the progress of the
Fascist legions, Premier Facta frantically urged him to declare martial law. But when the badly frightened Victor
Emmanuel learned that the army had refused to fight
against the Fascisti, he demanded instead the resignation of
the Facta government. Mussolini spent the morning at his
office in Milan awaiting a telephone call from Rome, which
finally came from the King's aide-de-camp, General Cittadini.
His Majesty desired Signor Mussolini to come to Rome to
form a new ministry.

"Stop the presses!" Mussolini shouted gleefully. "A new
headline, Arnaldo—MUSSOLINI NEW PRIME MIN-
ISTER!" Gripping his brother's hands between his own,
he added, "And put a new editor's name on the masthead—
that of Arnaldo Mussolini!"

Saying good-by to his wife and three children, Edda, Vittorio and Bruno, he promised to send for them as soon as
he could. To the crowd that turned out to cheer his flower-
decked train, he cried, "Tomorrow Italy will have a real
government, not just a ministry. The nation is in our hands
now, and we swear to lead her back into her ways of ancient
greatness!"

A tremendous reception greeted him at the railroad
station in Rome. A Fascist flying squad opened a path for
him through thousands of admirers who roared *"Alala!"*
and pelted him with flowers. Blackshirts ran beside and in
front of the car that drove him to the Royal Palace. Bands
playing martial airs welcomed him to the Quirinal which,
significantly, was already surrounded by armed Fascists.

Entering the Quirinal, Mussolini walked proudly down a
long marble hall toward the resplendently uniformed figure
on the jeweled throne. King Victor Emmanuel imperiously

extended his hand, studying him. Hesitating a moment, Mussolini brushed his lips against the royal fingers.

"Your Majesty must excuse my black shirt," he said gruffly, "but I come fresh from the battlefield. Thank God the battle has so far been bloodless. It will remain so if the three hundred thousand of my legions are permitted to enter Rome without resistance. They are now at the city's gates."

"Your legions are welcome in Rome," Victor Emmanuel said with as much dignity as the situation permitted. "But I will expect them to leave at the earliest possible moment."

The first legions entered Rome at dawn on the morning of October 30, 1922. At 3:00 P.M. there was a five-hour triumphal march led by Mussolini to the front of the Royal Palace.

"Mussolini!" roared the crowd. "Ayah, ayah! *Alala!*"

As the news flashed throughout the country, millions of Italians cheered the new strong man at the helm of the nation's destiny, confident Il Duce would solve all of their problems.

♦ 6 ♦

"ITALY IS MINE!"

Mussolini was impatient to begin wielding power as Prime Minister, but there was a ticklish job to be done before he could start remaking Italy. Fifty-two thousand Blackshirts, drunk on the wine of both victory and the vineyards, were surging through the streets of Rome. Many were in the great city for the first time in their lives, eagerly looking forward to a spree. Mussolini summoned the head of the State Railway Company. "It is now eight P.M. I give you exactly twenty-four hours to get every cohort of the *Squadristi* out of Rome."

"But, Excellency," protested the flabbergasted official, "that is impossible! Even in wartime it would take three days to move fifty-two thousand men in such a fashion!"

"Never use the word impossible to me. *Do it!*"

That night sixty military trains, some of them practically falling apart, were used to evacuate the Blackshirts from Rome. At 11:30 P.M. Mussolini turned to his exhausted Fascist General Staff and said exuberantly, "It's almost Wednesday. Time to begin today's Cabinet meeting!"

Events had moved him to the heights so quickly that he had to preside over this first Cabinet meeting in borrowed finery—a morning coat with too short sleeves, dress trousers too tight and too long, and Cesare Rossi's cuff links. He dismayed his followers by announcing that he was keeping for himself the portfolios of Prime Minister, Home Secretary and Foreign Minister. Then he stunned them further by announcing the context of his first decree—putting the Catholic church under state protection, forbidding all movements directed against it and making religious instruction obligatory in the schools .

"Why should anyone be surprised," scoffed Matteotti, the sharp-tongued Socialist deputy, "if a renegade to Socialism abandons his atheism to kiss the cross?" But Mussolini's purpose was crassly practical, not religious; he felt that he could consolidate power much more quickly by letting the church believe he was its protector, not its enemy, thus at least neutralizing its opposition until he felt strong enough to challenge its authority in Italian affairs.

He lost no time in letting his ministers know who was boss, and took a childish delight in dressing them down. Once he collided with a dignified bureaucrat on the staircase of the Viminale. The official, who until then had seen Mussolini only at a distance, snapped, "Clumsy fool!"

The new ruler of Italy stared at the official. "Who are you?"

"I am Deputy Alfredo Rocco, young man—Undersecretary of State for the Department of the Treasury!"

Mussolini put his hands on his hips and glared. "A government official? How *dare* you leave before closing time?"

Rocco gasped at this impertinence. "Who are you?"

"Your Prime Minister, you old fraud. You ought to be ashamed of yourself! Be at my office first thing in the morning for a lesson in the duties of a high official under Fascism!"

One month after taking power, he called a special meeting of the Chamber of Deputies. "I could have filled this dull, gray hall with corpses," he shouted arrogantly. "I could have nailed up the doors of Parliament and set up an exclusively Fascist government. You are sitting here only because of my generous gesture toward national unity. But understand my will to act must not be delayed for a second by useless oratory!"

Afterward ex-Prime Minister Nitti said gloomily, "Not a single man in the Parliament protested, and it was deeply sad and humiliating to witness that nobody dared to reply to this disdainful voice."

One of Mussolini's first official acts was to reward his Blackshirts by putting them on the state payroll as a National Guard, at the same time giving himself a disciplined private army of 150,000 Squadristi. To concentrate his power politically, he organized a Grand Council composed exclusively of Fascists, with himself as its head. In the first two weeks of its existence, the council was forced to meet thirty-two times, each meeting lasting for five or six hours, often until past midnight.

"A glutton for work" was the way Mussolini was described by the admiring United States Ambassador to Italy, Washburn Child, who urged the pale and worn Prime Minister, "Do take better care of yourself!"

Mussolini sighed dramatically, "It does not matter about me. The doctor has no right to be tired if he has to perform an operation!"

When his political opponents recovered from their first shock at the swift march of events toward dictatorship, many of them refused to remain silent or intimidated. Matteotti, aware of his sensitivity to ridicule, mocked him openly on the floor of Parliament.

Mussolini grimly vowed revenge. Borrowing an idea from the Russian Communists, he organized the Cheka, a secret police force charged with the task of violent reprisals against political foes, and headed it with the follower he trusted most, Cesare Rossi.

"I have to go to Lausanne for a foreign ministers' meeting," he told Rossi. "When I get back I want Cheka ready to act swiftly and expertly. Also, order an increase of Blackshirts in the National Guard to a total of half a million."

"Wouldn't that make them stronger than the King's Army?"

"Yes." Mussolini smiled tightly. "Wouldn't it?"

At the Lausanne conference Mussolini intended to force England and France to respect the right of the new Italy to an equal voice in the affairs of postwar Europe. He was personally delighted by a series of little ironies, marking his return to a Switzerland that had deported him seventeen years earlier as an undesirable agitator. Before his special train approached the border, the embarrassed Swiss government hastily ordered old police records on one Benito Mussolini conveniently "lost." He demanded and received the finest suite at Lausanne's elegant Hotel Beau Rivage, where he had once stood, faint with hunger, watching rich tourists dining and dancing.

From a wide window of his luxurious suite, Mussolini stared down at the Great Bridge he had once slept under as a vagrant. Turning to the Lausanne Chief of Police, who stood at his elbow, he could not help saying bitterly, "Today you stand at attention and honor me. Almost twenty years ago your police threw me into your miserable jail, and then ordered me out of your city!"

The Chief of Police, with the eternal blandness of the Swiss, shrugged philosophically. *"C'est la vie, Monsieur le Président!"*

Preparing to meet Lord Curzon of England and Premier Raymond Poincaré of France, Mussolini found himself suddenly a little dazed at realizing the heights to which he had climbed at age thirty-nine. He thought of Rachele's gasp when she had first heard the news: "You're the new Premier—*you*, Benito? Good heavens, how did such a fantastic thing like that happen?" He wondered secretly if, behind their dignified façades, other world leaders also felt a childlike private amazement that their daydreams had come true.

When he met Lord Curzon, he was very impressed with the veteran diplomat's poise and polish, and strove to emulate it. But he was also blunt about emphasizing that Italy was no longer willing to be just a tail to the Anglo-French kite. Curzon asked him what Italy's new foreign policy would be. Mussolini replied firmly, "Nothing for nothing!"

By agreeing to French occupation of the German Ruhr to enforce German war reparations, he won British and French recognition of Italy's right to Rhodes and the Dodecanese Islands as legal spoils of war. The Italians had already seized these islands illegally from the Turks ten years earlier. Now Anglo-French support guaranteed recognition of this power grab, helping to make the Mediterranean officially an Italian sea—"mare nostrum," as the Italians fondly called it.

This triumph inspired rumors that the King would award Mussolini the title of "Duke of Rhodes." But Il Duce, who scorned minor laurels, only said loftily, "It is better to arrive at one's goal unburdened by pointless honors."

Rachele continued to live with the children in Milan. Her husband told her lamely that he was so busy in Rome he would not be able to see them much anyway if they moved south; he would see them in Milan every chance he could get. Publicly he announced, "I shall not bring them to Rome, for I have no desire to make a family cult of the Mussolini name. One Mussolini is quite enough!"

In Rome he lived in a large apartment in the Palazzo Tittoni on Via Rasella, with a housekeeper named Cesara. No longer dressing the part of a revolutionary, he now wore uniforms elaborately trimmed in braid, business suits with stiff collars or cuffs, or diplomatic dress. But he never felt sure of himself in matters of dress. Once a friend who called to take him to a smart dinner party found him wearing tails with a black tie instead of a white one. When the mistake was pointed out, Mussolini fumed, "Well, then, *you* must wear a black tie, too, and we'll make the *others* at the party feel uncomfortable!"

The former peasant boy who had spent his formative years in and out of a dozen filthy jails found it more difficult to acquire habits of personal hygiene. He had to be reminded constantly to change his shirt and wear underclothes. It took a long time before he began bathing, shaving and cleaning his teeth daily. Once he outraged the Spanish king and queen by attending a reception for them wearing a two-day growth of beard. Smarting under their icy glances, he raged later to his housekeeper, "What am I supposed to be—an actor or a ruler!"

In addition to worrying about complexities of social life, he also feared making political blunders which might suddenly sweep him out of office. He had no real program to offer as yet. He had won Italy with shock waves of impassioned but empty oratory, making hundreds of vague promises without real meaning. Now his enemies pressed him to be specific about his plans for Italy.

"The imbeciles, Jesuits and Democrats incessantly demand a program of us," he fumed in *Il Popolo*. "The

Democrats of *Il Mundo,* do they desire to know our program? To break their bones—that's our program! And the sooner the better!"

However, he was shrewd enough to realize that such ill-tempered outbursts could not long postpone the national demand that he open Fascism's box of tricks. Every day in the Viminale, long before the first official arrived and long after the last had left, he paced his office thinking out a program.

A supreme realist, Mussolini had not forgotten for a moment that he had been restored as head of the Fascist movement only at the nod of Italy's powerful national association of industrialists and manufacturers. He had promised to destroy the labor movement, and knew that if he tried to renege they would quickly see that he was chastised by the antilabor Fascists of the Quadrumvirate.

At the same time he had to convince the Italian masses that he was the champion of the worker and peasant; that he was going to rectify all the wrongs they had suffered at the hands of the industrialists and landed gentry; that only he—not the Socialists, Communists, Catholics, Democrats or Liberals—could swiftly build them a paradise on earth.

"It's like trying to ride a horse in two opposite directions at once," he told Cesare Rossi. "But I think I know how. The capitalists claim they can make the country prosperous if they're allowed to run everything. All right, I'll give them a free hand. And I'll get the labor unions off their backs. No strikes will be permitted, in the public interest. Later all unions will be brought under government control."

Rossi looked incredulous. "The workers would revolt!"

"No, they'll *cheer* me, Rossi! You know why? Because it will be Il Duce, alone, who wins benefits for them! And I will excite them with thrilling speeches! I'll fill them with such national pride that they'll work harder for the glory of Italy! I'll give them parades, exhibitions, sport palaces! And I'll keep their bellies full—with jobs for all!"

Rossi grinned in admiration. "No one can beat the old Roman formula of bread and circuses!"

Mussolini began to pay off his debt to the economic rulers of Italy. He slashed taxes on big business, gave landlords a twenty-five-year tax exemption on every new building they put up, protected Italian industries against foreign imports by a high tariff, gave huge cash subsidies to Italian banks and trusts. To "win better service for the public," he handed over to private cartels businesses which the government had been operating—railways, post office, life insurance, telephone system, match manufacturing and municipal public utilities.

He also put a stop to two government activities which were upsetting rich Italians. An investigation into illicit war profiteering came to an abrupt end. So did the government program of land reform, whereby large estates were being broken up into small farms for poor peasants of the South.

Angry protests began to erupt in cities of the North as workers became more restless and suspicious. Mussolini summoned a delegation of Italy's most powerful industrialists to his office. "Gentlemen," he told them, "you must admit that up to now I have given you the kind of Italy you have always wanted."

"That's why you're here," one tycoon growled cynically.

"I'm prepared to do even more for you. But you must understand my plan and cooperate. I am going to pass a law establishing an eight-hour day and a forty-hour work week, with a minimum wage, for all workers!"

The industrialists looked thunderstruck. "Communism!" howled their spokesman wrathfully. In the Italy of 1923 an industrialist expected his laborer to work eleven to fourteen hours a day, six days a week, for starvation wages.

The Mussolini jaw tightened. "No, not Communism. *Syndicalism!* I will destroy the power of the labor unions to bargain for workers or pull them out on strike or stir them up against war. But the only way I can do this, to police and control the masses, is by convincing them that only the *government* can win benefits for them—not the unions!"

The leader of the industrialists grinned and put out his hand. "Mussolini, you're a genius!"

Shrewdly, he waited until a bitter attack had been made upon him in Parliament by huge Giovanni Amendola, a brilliant college professor turned deputy. "I say the workers of Italy should call a general strike," Amendola shouted hotly, "in protest against their betrayal by the Prime Minister!"

"My father was a village blacksmith," Mussolini thundered in reply. "I myself once earned my living with my hands, as a mason. Every fiber of my memory binds me to the workers of Italy! Is it possible any of you could seriously believe I should want to betray my origins? No, I fight only against those who want to deceive the workers, to thrust them down into the pit of eternal misery and poverty!" And then he threw his bombshell, introducing the new labor bill calling for an eight-hour day, forty-hour week, basic wage, fringe benefits and, in place of the right to strike, the "right to consult management." He followed this up by providing jobs for the unemployed through new government projects to widen harbors, build roads, erect public buildings. The economy began to boom, unimpeded by strikes.

Mussolini attended every new event that signaled economic progress, from the opening of a bridge over a creek to the launching of a merchant vessel. He made hundreds of soul-stirring speeches to inspire workers with a patriotic fervor to produce at top speed. "Go on—keep going on!" he would cry. "Stagnation is death!" He waged a furious campaign against bureaucratic sloth, fuming against trains which did not run on time, against post office clerks who moved too slowly. "Every branch of public activity and production must reach heights never touched before! There must be no such thing as the impossible!"

Privately he explained to Rachele, "If I don't keep hammering that idea into the heads of the masses, they'll just say that *everything* is impossible, and go back to sleep!"

He even pleaded with Italians to stop shaking hands and to greet each other instead with the Fascist salute. "It's not only more hygienic," he insisted, "but it wastes less time!"

Mussolini's first years in power were the golden age of Italian Fascism. Regimenting the working class, he built fine roads, schools, hospitals, bridges, low-cost homes, factories. Swamps were drained, railroads modernized, crop yields heightened. He introduced child and maternity welfare benefits, social security, housing projects, sanitation programs, water power projects. Many of the popular ideas which Mussolini pioneered were later copied by the democracies.

Mussolini continued to use *Il Popolo* as a trumpet for his ideas, with brother Arnaldo faithfully slanting the news to emphasize whatever Benito wanted played up. Significantly, despite the fact that Arnaldo was now in complete charge of *Il Popolo,* he never dared use Benito's chair or desk, which were always kept in readiness for the famous brother any time he dropped in during a visit to Milan.

The enemies of *Il Duce* found it useful to read *Il Popolo* to observe the foreshadowing of future events. When a Mussolini editorial fumed that a great, respected newspaper, *Corriere della Sera,* "should be treated as a Jesuit and as a scoundrel, and above all as a coward," it was no great surprise that the paper was bombed the same night. When *Il Popolo* raged against the 40,000-man Royal Guards as a "useless parasite created by Nitti," Blackshirts attacked Royal Guard units in a dozen cities and, in bloody street fighting, wrecked them as an organization. The King did not dare protest.

The Cheka now set to work systematically eliminating "the enemies of Italy" who opposed the Fascist program. The head of the Cheka in each town and city received from Il Duce a list of local citizens marked for assault, torture or assassination. All over Italy men were killed, in streets, in hospitals, in classrooms, in prisons, in churches and homes. Men were shot as they sat in the witness chair of a courtroom. If a political enemy fled into hiding, his son was killed in his stead.

Men were beaten up and left bleeding in the gutter simply for subscribing to an anti-Fascist newspaper. Public officials who had openly criticized Mussolini were stripped and marched naked through crowded city squares. Others were flogged, gagged with castor oil, crippled, blinded, thrown out of windows, forced into rivers up to their necks in midwinter.

Pope Pius XI, outraged and embittered by Fascist atrocities, addressed a message of protest to Mussolini. But Mussolini sent him a scornful, insulting reply, hinting that any meddling by the church in Fascism's affairs might result in retaliation by bloodshed and torch. The worried Vatican felt as helpless as the King to stop Italy's ruthless, Godless new leader.

Whenever foreign journalists dared to question Mussolini about the reign of terror going on with full police protection, his features darkened with indignation. "Don't exaggerate a few suicides by corrupt officials," he snapped, "or expect me to be responsible every time some hothead Fascist beats up a Communist or some other vermin! Compared to other countries, Italy is a model of law and order!"

Mussolini was careful to spare a few token enemies to whom he could point as proof that he did not assassinate his opponents. He confided to an English correspondent that a group of angry industrialists had wanted him to silence Amendola, but he told them, "Let him alone. Who knows how Amendola will think tomorrow? In the Mussolini of 1914, could you have seen the Mussolini of today?"

The more he grew to love the view from the heights of power, the more determined he became that no enemy would ever get the chance to overthrow him. Killing off his opponents through the Cheka became to him an intriguing kind of chess game, rather than the cold-blooded murder of human beings. And after all, wasn't the world a jungle where only the strong survived? What was it his father had told him when he was only a boy of seven? . . .

"To win respect, always carry a sharp knife and use it when you have to!"

THE MURDER OF MATTEOTTI

Enjoying public adulation, he barnstormed up and down Italy haranguing crowds to win popular support for the Fascist program. The more powerful capitalism became, he promised, the better off labor would be. He, Il Duce, would never let the bosses forget their obligation to the workers. Millions of doubtful Italians found themselves impressed and convinced by his supreme self-confidence, his eloquence, his magnetic manner. But even as he persuaded them to believe in him, he was too cynical about human nature to trust anyone else.

"Only a fool has faith in others," he scoffed. "If my own father were to come back into the world tomorrow, I wouldn't even trust *him!*" The deep suspicion in his soul was another reason why he felt driven to keep touring the country; that way he could keep a sharp eye on his opposition in each city.

Following the Romagna vendetta tradition of vindicating honor by settling old scores, Mussolini lost no opportunity to humiliate those who had ever offended him when he had been a nobody. His dark frame of mind was evident in five significant words he wrote in his autobiography: "Italy needed what? An avenger!" To avenge his expulsion as a youth from the Instituto Magistrale in Forli, he decided that this college, one of Italy's oldest and most respected, should be shut down. The municipality of Predappio, which had once refused to employ him as its town clerk, was demoted to the status of a village. His birthplace, Dovia, was promoted to the new municipality of Predappio.

He enjoyed visiting towns where he had lived and worked, accepting acclaim as the boy who made good. Suspicious, however, that old friends would capitalize on their former relationship, he preferred simply to wave to them from his police-escorted car. "It's astonishing how many old war comrades have come to life," he said sarcastically, "to remind me that they had carried me from the mortar pit where I was wounded to the dressing station. The number has now reached four hundred!"

High government and military officials were made to regret any supercilious attitude they had shown to Italy's new leader when he had been simply "that fellow Mussolini." He summoned and dismissed them like servants, keeping them standing as he sat, speaking to them with open contempt. He enjoyed making them run behind him for miles "because leaders of the nation should set an example of physical fitness," laughing cruelly at the utter exhaustion of the fatter dignitaries.

Wary of the potential threat of Gabriele D'Annunzio as a rival for power, because the public still revered him as a popular if eccentric idol, Mussolini sought to keep him bemused in retirement at Gardone with gifts of a private seaplane, cannons, a speedboat and other costly toys. He ordered the government to publish a forty-four-volume edition of D'Annunzio's writings, and blandly wired, "We remind you that what Italians expect from you is— poetry." Angered by the veiled warning to keep off the political stage, D'Annunzio replied dramatically, "No one shall influence me! I ask you to free yourself of the false politicians who are misleading you about me. Fie on you! Didn't your Fascist movement generate from *my* spirit? How can I be your enemy?"

When Mussolini worked out a treaty with Yugoslavia that allowed Italy to annex Fiume, D'Annunzio, "the hero of Fiume," once more came into the limelight. Mussolini moved swiftly, awarding him the title of Prince of Nevose, as well as Honorary General of the Air Force. Then as a further token of "respect," he sent D'Annunzio a special "aide," Commissar of Police Giovanni Rizzo, whose real function was that of jailer and spy. D'Annunzio was kept a prisoner in his own palace.

Mussolini also began taking bolder steps to silence growing thunder on the left, as Socialists, Freemasons, labor union leaders and liberal journalists joined forces in the fight to preserve what was left of freedom in Italy. In March, 1923, Mussolini openly attacked liberty and democracy. "For my part," he cried, "I prefer fifty thousand rifles to five million votes! I still believe firmly that Parliament is an infectious sore that poisons the blood of the nation. There is only one way to deal with malcontents who are a danger to the state—*force!* A party in power has the duty to defend itself against all. We Fascists throw poisonous ideas about liberty on the rubbish heap. Italians are tired of liberty—they have had an orgy of it! They want and need Order, Hierarchy, Discipline. Fascism has already stepped over the putrid body of the Goddess Liberty once. We are prepared to do so again!"

The more Mussolini struck out in all directions against those he suspected of plotting against him, the more fearful he became of reprisals. Never fully trusting anyone, he began to rely more and more on advice he had received almost twenty years before and had never forgotten. "I see you in a beautiful palace. Greater than a king you are," old Giovanna had croaked. "But you are surrounded by dangers, within and without. Listen to no one—only to the instincts of your own blood!"

He became more superstitious with each passing month, even making mysterious gestures in public to "ward off the evil eye." Motoring toward Rome along the Appian Way on New Year's Day, 1923, he saw a shooting star and babbled happily for days about this "auspicious omen." When quarreling Fascist aides came to him to settle their disputes, he decided the issue by studying samples of their handwriting.

In January, 1923, a visiting Middle East diplomat presented him with an Egyptian mummy as a gift, and he had it set up in a place of honor in the Palazzo Chigi, which he used as his Foreign Office. One midnight a week or so later, perusing the London *Times,* he read an article describing the evils that had befallen those who had violated the tombs of the Pharaohs. Perspiring with fear, he rushed to the phone and woke up half of Roman officialdom with frantic demands that the mummy in the Palazzo Chigi be removed from Rome with all possible speed.

He loved to visit a Capri fortune-teller named Madame Carmen to have his palm read, and often based important political decisions on what she saw in his future. Once she made him uneasy by warning that something was going to happen in June of the following year which would threaten his whole career.

To relax from the tensions of dictatorship, he often drove cars at top speed and stunted in airplanes. Weekends he spent at the garden-rich Villa Torlonia, where he kept a thoroughbred horse on which he galloped recklessly. An opponent in the Roman Senate once compared his passion

for daredevil riding to his leadership of Italy. "Why do I
love to fly on horseback?" he replied. "Because I'm young—
that's why! Be patient! Youth is a sickness of which one
becomes cured a little more each day!"

In September, 1923, when an Italian general was killed
during a military mission to Greece, Mussolini used the
incident as a pretext for his first experiment in imperialism.
He suddenly ordered the Italian Fleet to put seven thousand
men ashore on the Greek island of Corfu and seize it. When
the Greek protest against the Corfu seizure was supported
by Switzerland, he demanded angrily, "How can a nation
which hasn't fought for seven centuries judge a nation
which lost six hundred thousand dead in four years?"

His political enemies attacked him for taking Italy to the
brink of war on a flimsy pretext. "The nation which rules
war out as a last resort is lost!" he flared back. England,
worried about a disturbance of the status quo in the Mediterranean, told Mussolini to get his troops out of Corfu and
promised that the Greek government would meet his demands for reparations.

Secretly relieved, Mussolini hastened to comply. In victory
speeches to Italian crowds, he shouted proudly, "Whose is
the victory? Whose is the glory?"

"Ours!" the crowds roared jubilantly.

Although he loved their applause and cheers, he never
lost his secret contempt for the masses as a mindless mob.
"They're nothing but a herd of sheep," he once declared,
"incapable of ruling themselves. They need faith not reason.
Sometimes I feel the same disgust a sculptor does for the
clay he's modeling. But everything depends upon one's
ability to control the masses like an artist!"

He had very little respect for the man at the very pinnacle of the Italian nation, Victor Emmanuel. "The King is too small a man for an Italy which is on the road to greatness," he confided contemptuously to intimates. Once when the King annoyed him by being too inquisitive about his manipulations, Mussolini snarled to Cesare Rossi, "If he keeps on interfering, I just might change Italy from a monarchy to a republic!"

In 1923 he began a program of superhighway construction that added to his prestige among the Italian people, who were already grateful for steady jobs, labor peace, new schools and museums, and trains that ran on time.

Mussolini now felt sure enough of himself to take over the government as an absolute dictatorship. Should he simply sweep all parties except the Fascists out of Parliament? But if he seized power that crudely, without any pretense of popular support, he knew other heads of government would look down their noses and regard him as little more than a bandit. He had to show the world that Italians really *wanted* him as their Duce.

"Voting is a childish game," he scoffed. "It has humiliated our nation for decades." Nevertheless he called special elections in the spring of 1924, certain that he could count on the votes of millions of satisfied Italians. To ensure a clear majority, he ordered Rossi to see to it that the Cheka guaranteed his victory at the polls of every city. Opposition leaders who tried to hold election meetings for their candidates found their halls invaded by Blackshirts who stormed the platforms and blackjacked the speakers. Cheka thugs intimidated citizens at the polling places with threats of death for those who cast anti-Mussolini votes. Ballot boxes were stuffed, and Fascist Boy Scout troops were turned out en masse to vote as often as necessary.

Despite all the murders, assaults and frauds, two million votes were cast against Fascism, but according to Blackshirt election officials, Mussolini received five million votes.

He toured Italy in triumph. Hailed everywhere by crowds carefully rounded up for him by local Fascisti, Mussolini began to believe in his own legend. Accepting slavish adulation as his due, he scowled back at the cheering masses to project a public image of awesome grandeur. He drew more and more aloof even from colleagues closest to him, often standing in icy isolation at social gatherings, frowning at anyone who dared address him first. "I was prepared for my present position by a life that has always been lonely," he once explained gloomily. "I cannot live in any other way." He also felt that a man destined to become a demigod could afford "no intimate friendship and a minimum of personal feelings."

Following his rigged election victory, Mussolini's political enemies, aware of his plan to use the election as a pretext for ending parliamentary government and seizing total power for Fascism, decided the time had come for a showdown. Five major opposition parties chose the most eloquent spokesman among them to challenge Mussolini to his face with his crimes—Il Duce's old enemy, the popular and courageous Socialist deputy, Matteotti.

Matteotti created a public sensation by hurling damning accusations at Mussolini in Parliament, producing proof in the form of court findings, police records, news reports from the impartial *Corriere della Sera,* and even quoting from Mussolini's own mouthpiece, *Il Popolo.* He listed the shocking crimes of the Cheka; Mussolini's secret deals with the big industrialists to handcuff the unions; the assaults, murders and frauds at the ballot boxes. Roars of protest came from the Fascist benches.

Presiding over the Chamber, Mussolini raged, "Silence! That's enough, Honorable Matteotti! Do not provoke scenes!"

"The scenes are being provoked by *your* followers, Mr. Prime Minister, not by me!" Matteotti shouted defiantly. "I insist upon my parliamentary right to tell Italy the truth!"

When that day's session was over, Matteotti was acclaimed jubilantly by his colleagues. "It might be more appropriate," he smiled wryly, "if you saved all that flattery for my funeral oration in the Chamber." Next day *Il Popolo* carried an unsigned editorial warning: "Matteotti, vulgar charlatan, notorious scamp, ruffian of the worst sort, will do well to look out for himself. If one day he finds himself with a fractured skull, fractured in a good cause, he will not have any right to complain!"

The paper sneered at Matteotti's charges. A million and a half fraudulent Fascist votes? "We would have won just the same!" The opposition's public meetings had been smashed? "Such meetings are useless anyway!" Some "over-zealous Fascist patriots" had murdered political foes? "It is essential for enemies of the state to live in fear!"

But Italy's non-Fascist papers were headlining the scandalous charges Matteotti was hammering home in Parliament day after day. The foreign press carried the story on its front pages, giving Mussolini an international black eye as an election thief and political terrorist. Wild with rage, Il Duce bitterly regretted his mistake in not having crushed the opposition sooner. Now it would be difficult to silence Matteotti with the spotlight of the world upon him.

All through early 1924, Matteotti, joined by other opposition members, continued his slashing attack on the Mussolini regime.

"Fascism is no better than Bolshevism!" one deputy shouted. "You claim to save us from slavery only to enslave us!"

Mussolini lost his temper. "We were wrong not to imitate the Russians!" he shouted. "If we were the same as they, you would not be here now. You would be in jail where you belong!"

"We've just come from there!" yelled a Communist M. P.

"You would also have a bullet in your spine!" Il Duce raged. "You think we don't have the courage? Just wait! Your reward will come sooner than you think!"

"Italy cannot be ruled by threats!" Matteotti flung back.

The meeting broke up in a wild uproar. Afterward, Carlo Silvestri, a journalist, interviewed Cesare Rossi, who was beside himself with fury over Matteotti's attack on the Cheka.

"If he knew what was going on in Mussolini's head," Rossi fumed, "he would shut up! With traitors like Matteotti the only thing to do is let the revolver speak! Mussolini does not make idle threats. Nobody should know better than Matteotti that Mussolini needs frequent bloodshed to remain on top!"

But Matteotti let it be known that his final blast at the Fascists would be the most searing of all—one he hoped would shock the whole nation into rising up against Mussolini.

On a rainy Wednesday night, as Matteotti left his house, a car with five men screeched down the street and stopped beside him. The men jumped out, swung fists and clubs, dragged him struggling into the car and drove off. When

Parliament opened next morning, June 3, he did not appear to deliver his speech. He was still missing nine days later. Outraged whispers of foul play swept through Italy like wildfire.

Cesare Rossi called on Mussolini the morning of June 12 with a top secret report. The Cheka kidnappers, he related, had been led by Amerigo Dumini, an American-born gangster who liked to introduce himself as "Dumini—eleven murders." The other four terrorists were Volpi, Poveromo, Malacria and Viola, all hardened criminals with prison records. Matteotti had continued to fight them desperately as the kidnap car fled from the heart of Rome, and they had to stab him. The assassins had buried him twelve miles outside of Rome. Dumini had brought Rossi the dead man's bloodstained clothes, passport and other papers found on his body. Rossi now calmly opened his briefcase and exhibited these trophies to Mussolini.

"You fool!" raged Il Duce. "You've done me more harm than my worst enemies! Who told you to *kill* him?"

"But I thought . . . we agreed . . ."

Mussolini smashed his fist on the desk. "A fractured skull to shut him up, yes! Murder, no! You idiot, this is going to bring the whole world crashing down on our necks!"

His secretary Fasciolo brought him word that Signora Matteotti had come to Parliament hoping that one of her husband's colleagues might know what had happened to him. Thinking fast, Mussolini rushed out of his office to speak to her.

"Signora," he said in a voice of deep compassion, "I am having Rome turned upside down to find your husband for you. We know nothing certain yet, but there is still some hope that we will be able to restore him to you alive."

Rushing back to his office he snarled at Rossi to circulate

rumors that telegrams had been received from Matteotti in
Austria, where he had "gone for a Socialist conference."
That evening, at 7:30 P.M., Mussolini told the Chamber
of Deputies with great earnestness, "I hope that Honorable
Matteotti will shortly be able to resume his place in
Parliament."

A few days later Matteotti's body was discovered. Shocked
indignation swept over Italy. Everyone knew that he had
met his death at the hands of the Cheka, and why. Crowds
gathered every night outside the Palazzo Chigi to stare at
Mussolini in hostile silence as he left to go home. A storm
of protest began to mount in Parliament, in the press,
overseas.

Shaken, suddenly fearful that the Matteotti affair might
blast him out of office, Mussolini ordered the arrest of
Dumini. "Somebody must pay for this stupidity!" he raged.
He ordered Fasciolo to see to it that the gangster kept his
mouth shut, in return for which he would have to spend
only a little time in prison until the excitement died down.
The other four murderers were to be given funds to flee
the country.

But the sacrifice of one pawn could not stop the rising
storm of protest. Posters with Mussolini's picture were
ripped down or painted over with the word "Assassin!"
Cardinal Maffi of Pisa wired, "As a priest I weep; as an
Italian I am ashamed." The *Corriere della Sera* demanded
that Mussolini resign immediately. England's Labor party,
presided over by Prime Minister Ramsay MacDonald,
passed a resolution condemning Fascism for the murder of
Matteotti.

Mussolini felt the ground shaking under his feet. His
gloom and anxiety became intense as he remembered the
warning of Madame Carmen, the Capri fortune-teller, that

June would bring an upset which would threaten his whole career. Was the Matteotti affair the beginning of the end for him? Were all his dreams of glory to turn to ashes in his mouth?

Deeply depressed, he saw himself once more a penniless outcast wandering in wretched exile through Switzerland. Fear made him so nervous that he took to biting his finger-nails and at times felt such despair that he fell to the floor weeping, beating himself on the head with his fists. There was no help for it, he told himself bitterly. He would have to resign before all of Italy rose up in wrath and hurled him ignominiously on the scrapheap of history.

• 8 •

DUCE AND DEMIGOD

Fascists of the extreme right wing grew impatient with their leader's loss of nerve. One of them snapped at him, "Let's all go to prison, or let's *do* something to keep out of it! Which is it to be?" Mussolini whined, "What do you expect me to do with a corpse under my feet?"

He decided to make one last desperate attempt to appease the opposition by sacrificing some of his hierarchy. Cesare Rossi and Filippo Filipelli, head of Rome's Fascist paper, were arrested and jailed, and General De Bono, Fascist Chief of Police, was forced to resign. "Nobody can doubt the sincere horror of the government at this crime," Mussolini pleaded with the opposition in Parliament. "It is worse than a crime; it is a blunder. The whole nation recoils with the greatest horror from such an outrage. I assure you we have arrested, and are arresting, everyone on whom the faintest shadow of suspicion rests!"

Amendola, taking Matteotti's place, led the five chief opposition parties out of Parliament in a mass boycott of the government. This won them the name of Aventino, after the plebeians of ancient Rome who retreated from the city to the Aventine hills to stage revolutionary demonstrations against government tyranny. "The Aventino is guilty of secession, revolution!" Mussolini raged, indignant at the half-empty benches of Parliament. "Their act is unconstitutional!" Amendola kept the Aventino out for weeks, hoping that the King would feel compelled to act and force the Fascists to resign. But Victor Emmanuel remained cautiously silent.

Reflecting this tension and indecision, wild street fighting broke out in many cities between Blackshirt Squadristi and anti-Fascists. The uproar grew greater when Cesare Rossi, angry at being made a sacrificial goat, provided the Aventino with a confession of Fascism's crimes, listing over fifty murders and assaults ordered or suggested by Mussolini, in addition to the assassination of Matteotti. "Since Mussolini abandoned, accused and vilified me," Rossi wrote, "I no longer have any duty to remain faithful to him or conceal the truth."

"A tissue of lies and libels!" Mussolini raged when Rossi's confession was reported in non-Fascist papers all through Italy, as well as in the foreign press. He now became so deeply depressed that he seemed paralyzed as a ruler, and consternation spread through Fascist circles.

"You can go under if you want to!" the leader of the Milan Fascists shouted at him. "But *we* do not intend to!"

One of the most dangerous Fascist leaders was Roberto Farinacci, nicknamed "Farinacci the Sadist" by his colleagues. "What we need," he snarled at Il Duce, "is a revival of the 1922 spirit. Violence and *more* violence, until these fools of the Aventino understand who rules Italy! Appoint me new head of the Cheka, and I'll show you how to end this Matteotti nonsense!"

Mussolini meekly gave him the job of General Secretary of the Fascist party. Farinacci promptly began a new reign of terror in which 16 anti-Fascists were murdered, 36 seriously wounded, 172 assaulted; 46 centers of opposition activity were smashed. The Aventino movement collapsed in terror. Mussolini, astonished and delighted to find that he had miraculously ridden out the storm, quickly regained his old arrogance.

On January 3, 1925, he told Parliament defiantly that Fascism would no longer collaborate with any other parties but would rule as a dictatorship. He also reasserted his claim to sole leadership of the Fascist party.

"If Fascism is an association of evildoers," he challenged, "then I, myself, am the chief of these evildoers, and I boast of it! If Fascism has only been castor oil or a club, the blame is on me! If Fascism has been a criminal plot, if violence has resulted from it, the responsibility is all mine, because I deliberately created this atmosphere with my propaganda!"

He waited for over a year until he had consolidated his control of the army, militia, press and courts before permitting the five murderers of Matteotti to be brought to trial. Counsel for the defense was none other than Farinacci himself, who contemptuously argued that Matteotti had been a "traitor" and that he had not been assassinated but only "executed." Dumini, the chief defendant, brought laughs when he testified with a straight face: "We were riding along peaceably when suddenly Matteotti developed TB and died of a hemorrhage."

Despite medical testimony that Matteotti had been stabbed thirty-seven times, Dumini, Volpi and Poveromo were found guilty of "unintentional" homicide, sentenced to five years in jail and freed a few weeks later when Mussolini decreed an amnesty for political offenders. Viola and Malacria were acquitted. As for Rossi, he was allowed to escape to France on condition that he promise to remain silent about the affair.

Foreign journalists were not allowed to report the sordid

whitewash of the Matteotti case to their papers overseas. "It would have meant arrest," explained *The Chicago Tribune* correspondent later, "and expulsion from Italy."

Since Amendola had now inherited the mantle of spokesman for the opposition, it was only natural that Mussolini should do all that he could, short of murder, to silence him. The defiant leader was attacked and mercilessly beaten twice in 1924, twice in 1925.

Mussolini now lost no time in tightening the reins of power. He put the Army, Navy and Air Force under his personal command, and took the first opportunity to dump Farinacci as party secretary. The Fascist leader who had saved his political skin commented bitterly, "To Mussolini every obstruction is just another springboard from which he can jump further!"

Italy began to taste the bitter fruit of terrible new laws. Citizens were sentenced to up to three years in prison for criticizing Il Duce, his decrees or his purposes. Suspected "enemies of the state" were thrown into prison by Fascist tribunals. Janitors were required by law to spy on tenants and report "suspicious behavior." Police and the National Guard broke in and searched homes at will.

It was hardly surprising that pictures of Mussolini began to occupy carefully prominent places in every home or that "VIVE DUCE!" was hastily painted in giant letters on mountaintops overlooking the picturesque towns and cities of Italy. Drunk with the intoxication of total power, he encouraged the slogan, "Mussolini is always right," and it became mandatory to address him as "Duce." Even Rachele timidly referred to him as "Il Duce," and later on his grandchildren were taught to call him "Grandpa Duce."

Italy's press dutifully glorified every new "Mussolini triumph"—the construction of steamers which could make

Naples to New York in five days; enlarged harbors at Genoa, Naples and Palermo; Alfa-Romeo cars and textiles that were winning world markets for Italian exports; artificial lakes and dams yielding electric power; the repair of ancient monuments; modernization of the railroads; reclamation of swamplands; the elimination of unemployment through public works. There was, indeed, plenty to cheer about, and Mussolini saw to it that the cheers were prompt and in chorus.

With no voice now daring to oppose him, he made himself master of Italian industry and rearranged the nation's economic system. The rich had little reason to complain. He organized Italy's industries as monopolistic cartels, free of competition, and guaranteed markets, prices and profits. Labor unions were transformed into "syndicates," without the power to strike, humbly dependent on the government for working conditions.

To keep Italy's workers pacified Mussolini organized the institution of the Dopolavoro—a labor club movement which provided sports, entertainment of all kinds, open-air movies, art studios, exhibitions.

"The people are ignorant children who must be taught, directed and looked after," Mussolini said contemptuously. "Besides, if we don't control their leisure for them, they'll just use it to organize back-room plots against us!"

He gave Italian workers Saturdays off to enjoy the events at the Dopolavoro centers that sprang up all over the country between 1925 and 1928. Mussolini used these "Fascist Saturdays" as opportunities to inflame patriotic feeling and a warlike spirit, especially in the young. Coining the motto, "Book and gun—perfect Fascist," he put schoolchildren from six to sixteen in a Blackshirted juvenile militia called the Balilla. With knives in their belts, they drilled and marched, yelling in chorus with adult troops. He encouraged them to participate in combative sports designed to keep them physically fit and aggressive. There were medals for tug-of-war, rowing races, pushball, fencing, boxing, wrestling. Teen-age boys were inspired to show off their martial spirit in roller-skating rinks by speeding headlong at each other, arms extended like lances in a jousting tournament, until the collision sent one of them flying off his feet to the concrete, sometimes headfirst.

The higher Mussolini's prestige soared, the more grandiose his plans became. Like the emperors and Pharaohs of old, he tried to ensure immortality for himself by building impressive monuments that would last down through the ages. He began to reshape the face of Italy with new Fascist buildings erected in "the architecture of the future"— straight, soaring lines of white granite and glass. These structures did, indeed, influence what we know today as "modern architecture."

"In five years Rome must appear wonderful to the whole world, enormous, orderly and powerful, as she was in the days of the first empire of Augustus," Mussolini told the Senate. He built the impressive Forum Mussolini, a giant stadium with over fifty huge statues of athletes in virile poses completely encircling the top. He was vainly confident that he was creating an immortal niche for himself in world history and that statues of himself would stand forever side by side in museums with the Napoleons, the Roman Caesars, even the demigods of ancient Rome. It was said of Mussolini that no public figure in the world up to that time had ever arranged to have himself more widely photographed, painted, sketched and sculpted.

Overseas visitors coming to see the new Italy were flooded with pamphlets singing Mussolini's praises in the most extravagant terms. Every new edifice was "conceived by the genius of the Duce," who was "heir to the glories of the Roman civilization." They were reminded over and over again that "the new and beautiful Rome the world admires is the Rome of Mussolini."

The new Fascist façade of beautiful buildings was erected in tourist areas of cities to impress visitors. But behind the façade, millions of Italian families continued to live in the same age-old poverty and misery, many crowded into grimy, cavelike single rooms, without light, heat, water or plumbing. Ragged Italians gave each other haircuts outside their front doors. In alleys choked with the smell of garbage and open sewage naked, dirty children played and begged, chickens fluttered, old women went by bent under backbreaking loads. This, too, was part of Il Duce's "proud new Italy"— in the back streets that tourists rarely saw.

Those Italians who found themselves better off under Mussolini, as well as those brainwashed by Fascist propaganda into thinking they were, roared their approval whenever Il Duce appeared in their midst. But the higher he climbed as a Caesar, the more out of touch he grew with the masses from which he came. He also drew increasingly aloof from his colleagues, who were made nervous by his impulsive rages, sudden suspicions, merciless scorn and swift changes of mind.

He was convinced, with good reason, that there were many who hated him enough to try to assassinate him. American journalist Lincoln Steffens reported that once Mussolini had attended a diplomats' conference with a revolver in his pocket, and his hand on the revolver. "History warns that dictators are apt to be shot at," Il Duce told Steffens grimly. "So if a dictator is wise, he keeps his eyes open—and shoots first!"

His growing fear of assassination kept him from partici-
pating in the negotiations at Geneva that led to the famous
Locarno Pact, but he went to Locarno briefly to sign for
Italy. This was the treaty which temporarily reconciled
France and Germany, who were quarreling bitterly over
Germany's postwar borders. Under the pact, Germany agreed
to demilitarize the Rhineland and respect her neighbors'
borders, while France agreed to guarantee the security of
the Ruhr region of Germany occupied by France after the
war.

On November 4, 1925, a few weeks after Mussolini returned from Locarno, a first attempt was made to assassinate
him, as he prepared to review Italy's Armistice Day parade
from the balcony of the Palazzo Chigi. Waiting for him
at a window of a room in the Hotel Dragoni opposite was
a disgruntled Freemason named Zaniboni, disguised in the
uniform of an army major. However, before he had a chance
to fasten Mussolini in the sights of his Austrian rifle, police
broke in and arrested him. "He was a vulgar Socialist who
had been followed for a long time," Il Duce told foreign
correspondents.

In the national excitement that followed Zaniboni's arrest,
Mussolini published decrees outlawing both Freemasonry
and the Socialist party. The Socialists bitterly charged that
Zaniboni had been egged on to the assassination attempt by
one of the Cheka's *agents provocateurs,* to give Mussolini
a seemingly respectable reason for outlawing them and the
Masons. Il Duce had long sworn to destroy the Masons
because the order upheld individual liberty, opposed dictatorship and supported constitutional government. "Their
very life must be made impossible!" he told the Cheka.
Now the Masons' leaders were jailed and over a thousand
lodges smashed.

"Thus ends Socialist-Masonic audacity!" he announced happily.

Two other assassination attempts also failed, but a third did reach its target. The shot went squarely to Mussolini's heart, but this time he was wearing a bulletproof vest sold to him by a manufacturer in Vienna. The outraged mob seized and killed the wrong suspect—a fifteen-year-old boy.

"Be sure the whole world knows that the criminal has been lynched!" Mussolini snapped at his aides. "Assassins must realize that I have mystic protection against them. Nothing will kill me before my task is done!"

If there were some who wanted to take his life, there were also a unique few who wanted to copy it. One of these was an Austrian admirer in Munich who sent Mussolini a humble request for an autographed photo. The Italian leader contemptuously dismissed the letter as the unwelcome adulation of a small-time, crackpot imitator who had wild dreams of seizing power by copying Il Duce's tactics. Mussolini forwarded the letter to the Italian embassy in Berlin, attaching a terse note: "Please thank the above-named gentleman for his sentiments, and tell him in whatever form you think best that the Duce does not think fit to accede to his request."

The snubbed Austrian, proud and vengeful, swore that the day would come when the dictator of Rome would lick the dust off his boots, because as dictator of Germany the pupil would have become the master. Adolf Hitler never forgot either his humiliation or his vow.

At the end of 1925, Mussolini arranged a private religious ceremony in Milan to solemnize his marriage to Rachele. He didn't explain his real motive—a gesture of appeasement toward the Catholic church, which was furious because he

had wrecked the Catholic Boy Scout movement to swell the
ranks of his Fascist Balilla. When the Pope had protested,
Mussolini replied blandly, "The education of the younger
generation can only be carried on by the state. Leaving it
to the church violates the spirit of modern times."

On the other hand, he sought to win papal support for
Fascism by making other concessions such as ordering a
mass to be said at all public functions, restoring the crucifix
to all classroom walls, putting chaplains in the army, ordering salary increases for the clergy, returning to the church
some property seized by the pre-Fascist government and
declaring some religious festivals to be national holidays.
He astonished Arnaldo by confiding that he intended to
pay a visit to Pope Pius XI and even to kiss the Pope's
slipper.

"Are you turning Catholic, Duce?" his brother gasped.

Mussolini laughed. "I'd kiss the devil's slipper if he had
something I want! No, brother, it simply occurs to me that
I've been blind to the value of international Catholicism.
If the Pope agrees to a partnership, Catholic organizations
overseas can open the doors to Roman Fascism!"

When the Pope granted him an audience, Mussolini did,
indeed, pay his respects to the papal slipper. The Pope
raised him and said softly, "Repent, my son. All is not yet
lost for you. Do you think now you know what time it is?"

Mussolini blushed at the reference to the watch he had
borrowed in Switzerland to mock a priest at Lake Locarno.
"Today I no longer deny God by according him five minutes
in which to strike me dead as proof that He exists," he
replied smoothly. "I now know why I was not struck by
lightning. The church needed me!"

He worked out an agreement with the Vatican, called the
Lateran Concordat, which recognized Vatican City as an

independent state and Catholicism as the official religion of Italy. The treaty also indemnified the church for state-inflicted losses since the Italian republic had been formed in 1870. Even so, the Vatican remained unreconciled to Fascism as pagan in spirit, and the split between Mussolini and the church became wider with each passing year. He soon found it necessary to unleash the Cheka, which led brutal attacks on priests and church property.

The Pope's reply was calm, patient and to the point. "Nothing built on violence ever endures," he declared.

Although Mussolini had signed the Locarno Pact in 1925 to help stabilize peace among the major powers, his foreign policy never ceased to be expansionist. He was convinced that there was not room enough in Italy for at least a million of her forty million population and that the nation would continue to be Europe's poor relation until he could win colonies to absorb these surplus Italians. England and France had empires—why not Italy? What nation had a greater right than the direct heir of the mighty Roman Empire?

In 1927 Mussolini launched the new Italian imperialism by making a secret deal with the English that let him force King Zog of Albania to sign a "mutual defense alliance." That tiny country was turned into an Italian satellite without a single shot being fired, although King Zog kept his throne for another dozen years.

Speaking to his now almost wholly Fascist Parliament in May of that year, he declared that Italy must be ready to arm five million men swiftly. In 1928, making sure that Victor Emmanuel could not interfere with his plans, he stripped the King of the power to appoint future premiers, giving this power to the Fascist Grand Council he controlled.

To prove to the world that the Italian people were solidly

behind him in his bid for empire, he staged a national election in March, 1929. Fascist candidates won a sweeping victory, since there were no opposition candidates. Soon afterward he publicly denounced the Versailles Treaty, claiming that it had humiliated Italy, and swore revenge.

It was not until 1929 that Mussolini finally brought Rachele and their children to Rome, moving them into the Villa Torlonia, an estate offered them by a prince. By this time there were five children—Edda, Vittorio, Bruno, Romano and a new baby girl, Anna Maria. Their father spent most of his time at the Palazzo Venezia, which he used as both an office and bachelor's quarters. Cynics said he stayed at the Villa Torlonia only long enough to be photographed with Rachele and the children, to preserve his image as a family man.

Rachele had long since reconciled herself to playing only as much of a role in her husband's life as he permitted. She was aware that his rise to power had added steel to his nature, but she still found him capable of gentler moods. He was fond of the children when he was with them although he promptly forgot about them when they were out of sight. He soothed himself with the violin; he loved riding around the extensive grounds on horses presented to him by admirers. Rachele also observed without comment the signs that he did not groom himself for her alone. He drenched himself in Eau de Cologne and, when he began losing his hair, decided that women would find him more fascinating if he shaved his head completely.

In 1930 Mussolini's eighteen-year-old daughter Edda married Count Galeazzo Ciano, son of one of Il Duce's oldest and stanchest supporters. Always able to twist her father around her little finger, Edda saw to it that Ciano rose quickly up the ladder of Fascism so that in three short years the thirty-year-old Count was appointed Foreign Minister. He also endeared himself to his father-in-law by providing the first Mussolini grandson, Fabrizio.

The following year Il Duce was saddened by the loss of the only man he had ever fully trusted in his stormy life—his brother. Dutiful, quiet Arnaldo had been severely shocked by the sudden illness and death of his twenty-year-old son, an only child. Benito had insisted that he come to live at the Villa Torlonia, hoping that Rome would help his brother forget his sorrow more easily. But Arnaldo had lost his will to live and died in Benito's arms on December 21, 1931. For the first time since he had been a boy, Benito Mussolini cried. Anguished, he wept, saying to Rachele, "Only now that Arnaldo is gone do I realize how much I loved and depended upon him!"

• 9 •

IMITATOR IN BERLIN

The announcement of a Tenth Anniversary Celebration of Fascism in 1932 came as something of a shock to the rest of the world. Had Benito Mussolini already ruled Italy for a decade? The March on Rome seemed only yesterday. An overseas tribute came from the former American Ambassador to Italy, Richard Washburn Child, who declared emphatically, "The Duce is now the greatest figure of his sphere and time."

Millions of Italians, however, were beginning to have grave doubts. The Fascist government, unable to meet the cost of its public works program, had simply slashed wages. Men now earned less than ten cents an hour, making them the lowest paid workers in Europe. The Fascist National Academy published a scientific paper revealing that Italians weren't getting enough to eat. Mussolini assured the Chamber of Deputies with a shrug, "Fortunately the Italian people are not yet accustomed to eating several times a day. Since they have a modest standard of living, they don't feel want and suffering very much."

Workers in the cities were too carefully policed by the Cheka (now legalized as the OVRA with over 100,000 secret and uniformed operatives) to protest. But peasants in the South of Italy staged violent demonstrations against heavy taxes. Shouting "Death to the famine-makers," they fought local police, sacked mayors' offices, ripped down pictures of Mussolini, burned him in effigy, smashed Dopolavoro buildings and chased tax collectors into the hills.

The deeply religious peasants had been inspired to revolt by a papal encyclical published from Paris, where it had been smuggled to escape censorship. The Pope told the world that Fascism and Catholicism were not and could never be the same thing. He denounced the Fascists for "indecencies, destruction, confiscation and vandalism." Behind this indignation lay the OVRA's grim record of twelve thousand secret arrests in five years. One foreign journalist whom Mussolini respected ventured to reproach him one day for such harshness.

"Who in my whole life has shown *me* tenderness?" he quavered in self-pity. "Nobody! I was brought up in a poor, horribly poor home, and my life has always been poor and bitter. Where could I have learned tenderness? At school? In church? In the world? No . . . *nowhere!* Then why do people wonder that I am reserved, solitary, harsh and stern?"

He grew more and more autocratic each year, hardening personal whims into laws. Shaking hands was forbidden; only the Fascist salute could be used for greeting. The press must not use the plural term "supreme hierarchies" because "the party has only one hierarchy—Il Duce!" All sketches of women drawn by artists and cartoonists must show them not slim but plump, to reflect Mussolini's private preferences.

The royal family of Italy, nervously aware that it was within the dictator's power to end the monarchy and send them into exile if the impulse seized him, were careful to ingratiate themselves by providing him with the use of their castles and hunting lodges for vacation retreats. Mussolini soon fell into the habit of snapping his fingers for anything he wanted or needed. He never bothered to carry money; if he wanted to dispense charity or tips there was always an attendant following him with a portfolio of lire. When he had an urge to fly, he summoned his personal bomber. If his mood was for the sea, a warship would steam up at his disposal. "Money is only important," he once explained, "when you don't have power."

He took great pride that, in the eyes of the whole world, Italy was Mussolini, Mussolini was Italy. When he struck virile and dynamic poses for the camera, he felt that he was personifying the spirit of the new Rome. Turning fifty in 1933, he refused to let Italy's press mention the fact, and would not let himself be photographed wearing the glasses he now needed. To demonstrate his vigor to journalists, he challenged Farinacci to a "friendly" duel. That Fascist official, still arrogant, was nevertheless wise enough to lose. Keeping himself fit by riding, swimming and tennis, Mussolini weighed himself anxiously every morning to make sure he hadn't gained an ounce.

In 1932, however, a new dictator began to steal the headlines from Mussolini. He was the product of a Germany which had suffered under twenty different cabinets since the Versailles Treaty had given birth to the weak Weimar Republic. Each cabinet had fallen, trying to cope with Germany's problems of huge war debts, unemployment, depression, political violence, anti-Semitism, sabotage by army generals and business tycoons, and such terrible inflation that it took a suitcase full of paper marks to buy a loaf of bread.

Adolf Hitler, fanatical ex-corporal of the Bavarian Army and an admirer of Italian Fascism, collected a group of psychopathic misfits around him in the beer halls of Munich to plot the overthrow of the Weimar Republic and seize

Germany for himself as Mussolini had seized Italy. Il Duce was indignant at the slavish way in which his Teutonic imitator copied every trick of Italian Fascism.

"What a clown this Hitler is!" he fumed to his son-in-law, Ciano. "Not an ounce of originality! I create the Fascist party emphasizing a nationally controlled socialism, so he calls *his* group the National Socialist party! He tells the Germans he's going to get rid of democracy to give them a revolution—exactly what I told the Italian people! Then he gets arms and money from the big industrialists by promising to destroy the labor unions—another Mussolini tactic!"

His son-in-law fed his indignation. "What about his putting his storm troopers in brown shirts, Duce—to imitate your Blackshirts? You create a secret police, the OVRA; he copies you with his Gestapo! And he deals with his political enemies precisely the way you did—by street violence!"

Mussolini's fist smashed down on his long carved desk. "There's no end to the beggar's gall! I invent the Fascist salute, so he copies it with a clenched fist salute. I use a fasces as my insignia; he selects a swastika. I stir up patriotic feel·ing with giant parades and rallies; he organizes parades and rallies! I create the Dopolavoro movement to make the young strong and fit; he talks about a Strength Through Joy movement for German youth! Ciano, I tell you if I started hopping around on one leg, that fool in Munich would begin bouncing around on his head!"

Coming to power as Chancellor in January, 1933, Hitler consolidated control of the government far more swiftly than Mussolini had been able to do. In a few months all of Germany was under rigid one-party rule. Hitler's storm troopers began to persecute German Jews just as Mussolini's Blackshirts had terrorized Italian Catholics and Freemasons. Il Duce was unenthusiastic and highly suspicious. Was

Europe big enough for *two* dictators, especially when one of them led an aggressive people always eager for war, as their history proved, unlike the Italians whose instincts were for peace and who had to be constantly whipped into a war fervor to keep them militant?

Ciano, Foreign Minister of Italy, offered shrewd advice to his father-in-law. "No matter what we think of this upstart or the danger he represents to Italy, his victory has propaganda value for us. Now there are *two* dictatorships in Europe—and two less democracies! Shouldn't our press play up Hitler's success as a triumph of the Fascist idea, of Il Duce's wave of the future?"

"My daughter didn't marry a fool!" Mussolini beamed, clapping him on the back. "But let's have no illusions between ourselves, Ciano. Fascism and Nazism are as different as day and night. We stand for the rights of the individual, of the church, of the family. The Nazis are barbarians who can only murder, loot and blackmail. We have *much* more in common with the Soviet Union!" He gave Ciano a sly glance.

Ciano looked startled. "Duce, does that mean that you intend to recognize Russian Communism?"

"Can you think of anything that would worry the democracies more? I'll surprise you even further, Ciano. I'm planning a treaty of friendship with Moscow!"

In the world struggle for power, Mussolini had decided, he would need any allies he could get. A treaty with Joseph Stalin would also strengthen his hand with the upstart in Berlin. Hitler would think twice about trying to swallow Italy if he knew that the moment he tried it he would find himself in the hug of the Russian bear. Mussolini was also willing to cooperate with the democracies in helping them curb Hitler, but at the same time he was ready to support Hitler whenever this would serve the best interests of Italy.

In Berlin, meanwhile, Adolf Hitler was being cautioned by some military advisers against relying on Italy to help his plans for world conquest. Wehrmacht staff officers warned him that Italy could never be trusted, and that the Italian Army was, in any event, worthless for offensive warfare. Nevertheless Hitler became uneasy when, in March, 1933, England's Prime Minister Ramsay MacDonald paid a visit to Mussolini in Rome, giving rise to rumors of a four-power pact that would unite England, France, Italy and the United States.

A few weeks later Hitler rushed two of his henchman to Rome. Franz von Papen and Hermann Goering urged Mussolini, as a "fellow dictator," to stay aloof from the democracies, to join Hitler in creating a Fascist Internationale at a Nuremberg Congress in the fall. By September Mussolini decided that he had more to gain temporarily by falling in with Hitler's plan, but he was careful not to do so too enthusiastically. He was impressed, the following month, when Hitler defied the League of Nations by taking Germany out of it and withdrawing from the International Disarmament Conference.

Early in 1934 Hitler felt ready to take over Austria as part of a Greater Germany, and quarreled with some military advisers who cautioned him that a march on Vienna might alarm Mussolini into armed opposition to protect Italy's borders. Il Duce was also a warm personal friend of Engelbert Dollfuss, the Austrian Chancellor. The German General Staff urged Hitler to pay a visit to Mussolini first and win his consent.

"What a joke!" Il Duce told Ciano grimly. "The German generals can't control that crazy hothead, so they've tipped me off that he wants to grab Austria, and hope that *I'll* knock some sense into his head by telling him no, I won't let him!"

The two dictators saw each other face-to-face for the first time in the Villa di Stra at Venice in June. They met in civilian clothes, but Mussolini quickly changed into Fascist uniform for a psychological advantage. He also assumed an aggressive stance—legs apart, hands on hips, chin thrust forward. By an odd "coincidence," too, whenever the two dictators were seen together in public, there were tremendous roars of "Duce! Duce! Duce!" but no cheers for Hitler.

The conference between them was anything but fruitful. Their only point of agreement was that the Versailles Treaty should be smashed and that Italy and Germany should jointly oppose the League of Nations. Apart from that, the two dictators spent much of the time shouting impatiently at one another. Mussolini insisted that Hitler should stop trying to terrorize the Dollfuss government through the Nazis of Austria; that persecuting the Jews of Germany was a blunder that would give dictatorship a bad name.

"Who are *you* to lecture me about persecuting minorities?" Hitler replied furiously. "Didn't you persecute the Masons? Besides, if you had taken the trouble to read *Mein Kampf,* you would have understood about the superiority of the Nordic races and the inferiority of the Mediterranean races!"

Mussolini bridled. "Do you mean Italians as well?"

"I mean *all* dark-skinned, dark-haired races!" Hitler snapped. "Jews, Italians, Greeks, Arabs—all the inferior races with Negro blood in their veins!"

Il Duce's eyes glittered at this outrageous prejudice. "You forget that when the Germans were only barbarians, the

Roman Empire in the Mediterranean was the center of world culture!"

"Culture!" snarled Hitler. "When I hear talk about culture, I have one impulse. To draw my revolver!"

Mussolini gave up in despair, knowing it was useless to try to civilize a man who understood nothing but violent politics, and who feared and hated intellectuals as men with dangerous ideas. Il Duce, who loved books, could not help feeling a deep contempt for a man who burned books in great public bonfires, but he forced himself to pretend amusement. "Ah, well," he said, "we can't all think alike, can we? Come on, let's cool off with a motorboat ride on the Grand Canal." When the German dictator had taken his place beside his host, Il Duce opened the throttle wide and sent the boat racing from side to side in a wild, leaping ride that left Hitler pale and speechless. Mussolini grinned slyly.

"It was the only time I could shut him up," he chuckled later to Rachele. "He's really quite mad. He has absolutely no self-control. Wild ideas spew out of his mouth, one after the other. And he's insanely obsessed with the German vice —anti-Semitism. Our meeting came to nothing. Perhaps it's just as well. With that German talent for stealing a good idea and ruining it, he's liable to give dictatorship a bad name!"

A month later he and Rachele were entertaining Frau Dollfuss, wife of the Austrian Chancellor, and their two children at a villa near their own in Riccione. They were expecting Dollfuss himself momentarily. Suddenly there was a diplomatic phone call from Vienna, with news that Austrian Nazis had broken into the Chancellor's office and assassinated him. They were appealing to Berlin for "anschluss" with Germany, asking storm troopers to march into Austria. With

Dollfuss out of the way, there was no symbol to rally Austrians to fight for their independence. Mussolini was furious.

"That scoundrel, Hitler!" he stormed. "*He* killed Dollfuss! And he had it all planned when he was in Venice with me last month! He's a dangerous madman who will have to be stopped before he plunges the whole world into war!"

Two Italian divisions were rushed to the Brenner frontier as a warning to Hitler not to move south into Austria. Il Duce hoped for at least verbal support from London and Paris, but those governments were evasive, apparently content to let Mussolini bell the cat. Bitterly, he told Rachele, "I expected more from our Western friends. They've let me down. Their apathy could encourage Hitler!"

The German dictator hesitated, committed to world conquest but not yet feeling himself militarily strong enough to risk war. He withheld the order to invade Austria, and Kurt von Schuschnigg, Austrian Minister of Justice, took office as the new Chancellor, restoring order under the protection of Italy. Mussolini, out of his dark suspicion of Hitler and close friendship with Dollfuss, found himself suddenly being hailed by the world as a champion of peace.

In Germany Hitler was moving swiftly to consolidate his power. When President von Hindenburg died in August, 1934, Hitler combined that office with his own as Chancellor into one supreme authority—*Der Fuehrer*, "The Leader." Early the following year he renounced the Versailles Treaty and ordered conscription of German men, in defiance of the treaty.

Mussolini observed with vexation that Hitler's stormy threats of aggression—a technique for bloodless conquest—

were winning terrified respect from the Western powers. Europe was entering a new period of appeasement when a dictator need only rattle his sword to frighten the democracies and have them come running with a bribe to persuade him not to unleash full-scale war. So Mussolini decided that it was the strategic moment for Italy to invade Ethiopia (formerly called Abyssinia), an acquisition which he felt would help solve his problems of where to relocate a million surplus Italians.

Summoning the French Foreign Minister to Rome, he hinted at his intentions. Pierre Laval, anxious to keep Mussolini in the Western camp, gave him soothing assurances that Paris and London would not seriously object to Italy's "peaceful penetration" of her "rightful sphere of influence in Africa." In April, 1935, there was a meeting in Stresa of England's Prime Minister Ramsay MacDonald and Foreign Secretary Sir John Simon with France's Premier Pierre Flandin and Laval, and Mussolini and Ciano for Italy, during which the three countries agreed to support the Versailles Treaty against any attempt by Hitler to change it by force. Mussolini returned to Rome in a jubilant mood, convinced that in return for his support, he had been given a free hand to make his move in Ethiopia.

He mobilized Italy's armed forces for the invasion. But new belt-tightening restrictions to prepare for war irked the Italian people. Peasants were grumbling openly, and university professors dared to speak out against the folly of a new military adventure in Africa. Mussolini grimly ordered mass arrests of intellectuals in Turin, Milan and other cities. The famous antiwar novel, *All Quiet on the Western Front,* was banned, and one Fascist paper told its readers, "Instead of reading superfluous books, read—and reread—the speeches of our great leader!"

Mussolini's generals were secretly worried about his decision to invade Ethiopia. Not only did they fear that because of world opinion this might force the League of Nations to take reprisals against Italy, but they were also alarmed because Mussolini intended to take direct charge of the army himself. Knowing he was a hopeless military amateur, they dreaded the worst. Mussolini refused to listen to any persuasion or warnings and raged to Agriculture Minister Rossoni, "Keep away those fools who are trying to stop me from listening to the instincts of my blood!"

• 10 •

EMPEROR BENITO

In London, Prime Minister MacDonald was worried, too, for fear that the Ethiopian crisis could destroy the League of Nations. He knew that Emperor Haile Selassie, as a member of the League, would demand protection. If the League failed to act, its prestige would be destroyed, but on the other hand if the League stopped Mussolini, he would be lost to the West and thrown into Hitler's arms. MacDonald decided to heed the suggestion of his Foreign Minister, Lord Simon, and try to buy Mussolini off from attacking Ethiopia by offering to give him the port of Zeila in British Somaliland.

Mussolini was furious when Anthony Eden, then a junior minister in charge of League affairs for the British, sped to Rome with this petty bribe. Il Duce's plans called for a glorious military victory, parades, snapping flags, blaring trumpets, roaring crowds, world excitement. He would show Hitler—and the whole world—a thing or two!

He received Eden's proposal coldly. "I've had quite enough of these territorial gifts at third hand. At the Stresa Conference it was understood that I was to have a free hand in Ethiopia in exchange for supporting the democracies against Hitler."

"But it was naturally expected," Eden protested, "that your penetration of Ethiopia would be peaceful."

"Peaceful! Who are the English to lecture me? A nation that conquered a world empire with its navy?"

"We are the British *Commonwealth* of Nations, sir. Each nation is free to make its own decisions, and need consult no dictator." As Mussolini glared at him, Eden asked, "Aren't you concerned that your Ethiopian adventure may lead to serious conflict with England?"

"I'm quite aware of that possibility!" Il Duce snapped. "Perhaps England had better think about it as well!"

The two men parted, and remained, mortal enemies.

A few months later Mussolini was ready. On October 2, 1935, he appeared on the balcony of the Palazzo Venezia in full-dress uniform. In words that rang throughout the nation from radio loudspeakers, he announced that Italy was declaring war on "the Ethiopian barbarians."

"Julius Caesar once dominated the world. Every stone around us here should remind us of that fact. We must believe that what was our destiny yesterday will again be our destiny tomorrow!"

Emperor Haile Selassie at once demanded that the League of Nations come to his rescue. However, Mussolini had secret support from Britain's generals and admirals, who admired him as much as they detested the disarmament policies of the League; and so because of their pressure, no military force opposed the Italian invasion of Ethiopia. To save face the League simply voted "economic sanctions" against Italy—a trade boycott. Yet Laval of France secretly assured him that Italy could still count on getting supplies.

Indignation against Mussolini rose in organized labor circles overseas. The British Labor party called for a "labor war" against Fascism, both Italian and German. The American Federation of Labor declared a boycott on goods from both dictatorships and denounced Mussolini for attacking

Ethiopia. On the other hand, Arnaldo Cortesi, Rome correspondent for *The New York Times,* informed Americans, "The people have become accustomed to the idea that war is not only inevitable, but also necessary for a solution of some of Italy's most pressing problems."

The commander chosen for Italy's mechanized Expeditionary Force was General De Bono, the former Fascist Chief of Police who had allowed himself to be fired as a temporary sacrifice in the Matteotti affair. "I will be your brains," Mussolini told him tartly. "You will move only as I direct!"

A huge map of Ethiopia was hung on a wall of the Villa Torlonia, and Mussolini spent much of his time moving little battle flags around it. He constantly changed his mind about tactics, telegraphing a stream of contradictory commands to De Bono, who became increasingly confused. The campaign against ill-trained Ethiopian troops with ancient weapons bogged down in rain and mud for two months. The world press began to laugh.

Furious, Mussolini replaced De Bono with his Chief of Staff, General Pietro Badoglio. As soon as Badoglio took the field, he showed common sense and courage by crumpling the telegrams from Rome and growling, "Rubbish!" Rolling back Selassie's forces with the precision of a military expert, he was soon threatening the Ethiopian capital of Addis Ababa. Mussolini, now alarmed that he was moving too fast, bombarded him with orders to halt. Badoglio dared to wire back, "Leave me alone if you want a victory!"

Mussolini received letters and wires of encouragement from Hitler, who was shrewdly using this gambit to pave the way for the Fascist alliance he needed before he could challenge England and France. The Italian dictator was wryly aware of the irony of a situation in which Hitler was supporting him despite Italy's opposition to Germany's designs on Austria, while despite Italian support of a pact London and Paris wanted, they had organized League sanctions against Italy.

In mid-November, Italy began to feel the pinch of the League's economic boycott. Mussolini appealed to the nation, and also to Italians in America, for donations of gold jewelry which could be melted down "on the Altar of the Fatherland." The Fascist press dutifully reported that the first gold wedding ring had been donated by Signora Rachele Mussolini, and the second by Il Duce himself. "What memories in this little yellow circle!" he sighed sentimentally as he gave Rachele his ring to surrender with her own. "Ah, well, we mustn't grumble at sacrifices for Italy!"

Staring at the rings in her palm, Rachele wondered if her husband's words concealed a double meaning. She had heard rumors about La Petacci, a beautiful young girl.

Claretta Petacci had been ten years old when the March on Rome had taken place, and ever since had slept with Mussolini's picture under her pillow. Unlike girls who worship film stars from a distance but outgrow their crush, Claretta never ceased to revere her idol even after marriage to, and separation from, her husband. Her dreams came true one day when she managed to meet Il Duce, who was attracted by her open adoration. He soon found himself falling in love with her. Romans began gossiping about the "Madam Pompadour of Italy."

To Mussolini, now fifty-three, Claretta offered an irresistible illusion of his own vanished youth. Warming himself in the infatuation of a girl thirty years his junior, he found in her a blessed escape from all of the grim worries that now clung to him like a drenched cloak—anxiety over the blunders in Ethiopia, fear of Hitler, new pain flaring up from his old stomach ailment, lonely isolation from all human warmth since the death of his brother Arnaldo.

When Edda angrily ventured to take him to task for his indiscretion, Mussolini told his daughter gloomily, "When you get to be my age, you won't be so quick to judge a man for seizing what happiness is left to him!"

The outcome of the Ethiopian war was never in doubt. Although Selassie had been able to raise an equal number of tribesmen to oppose the Italian force of 300,000 under Badoglio, only one Ethiopian in twenty was armed with a rifle. Mussolini fretted when bad weather and worse roads held up victory. At an anniversary celebration of the founding of Rome, he wanted to announce that Rome had once more become an empire. "Give me complete victory by April 21," he wired Badoglio impatiently, "No matter how many casualties it costs, no matter how ruthless you have to be to force the enemy to surrender."

Sweden protested bitterly when Italian planes bombed and strafed Swedish Red Cross tents near an Ethiopian encampment. One Italian paper scoffed, "Should Italy's aviators fill their bombs with cologne water, or first drop lookouts by parachute to make sure no Swedish doctors are in the area?" Italian artillery began firing mustard gas shells, causing 30,000 casualties among Selassie's troops. Italian infantry used soft-nosed dumdum bullets, outlawed by the Geneva Convention because they produce dreadful septic wounds. The Ethiopian Emperor, abandoned by the League of Nations he had believed in and trusted, decided in desperation to fight fire with fire. He procured dumdum bullets for his own troops, and the tribesmen took savage revenge against Italian soldiers unfortunate enough to fall into their hands. With an air of outraged innocence, the

Italian press spluttered, "Bandits in Ethiopia are attacking brave Italian soldiers, and subjecting prisoners to all sorts of barbaric indignities!"

Badoglio was ten days late in delivering the total victory Mussolini demanded. On May 1 Haile Selassie escaped from Addis Ababa aboard a British cruiser, and Mussolini announced the end of the war. Told proudly by Badoglio that the whole campaign had cost them only 1,500 dead, Il Duce was annoyed. "Too few sacrifices for our own good!" he complained. "If you had moved faster, with heavier casualties, we would have had a more impressive performance —and an empire dignified by the price of a respectable amount of Italian blood!" Official jubilation was in order, however, to signify the conquest of Ethiopia as a major triumph, so Badoglio was appointed Viceroy of Ethiopia and Duke of Addis Ababa.

Mussolini was credited by political observers with having won for Italy not only a colony to absorb its surplus population, but also a rich source of raw materials—coffee, hides, ivory, tobacco, bananas, gold, platinum, potash, coal, sulphur, phosphate. As time went by, however, Mussolini glumly realized that it was costing Italy more to develop these resources than she was earning from them. The Ethiopian adventure added up to a net loss, although this fact was carefully kept out of the Italian press, especially since in March Hitler had scored another bold triumph by reoccupying the demilitarized Rhineland zone, in defiance of the Locarno Pact.

On May 5, Il Duce appeared on his balcony to proclaim that Italy was now no longer just a kingdom but an empire and that many great new conquests lay ahead. "The days of the Caesars are once more at hand!" he shouted to a storm of cheers and applause. There were cries of "Duce

Emperor! Duce Emperor!" Mussolini pretended to ignore
them, but his large eyes glowed as voice was given to his
secret aspirations. He knew that the cries were also being
heard in the Villa Savoia by a worried King Emmanuel.

Pressure applied to the Vatican produced a reluctant state-
ment from Cardinal Pacelli, the Papal Secretary of State
(later Pope Pius XII), who hailed Mussolini as "a most
cultured restorer of Imperial Rome." Posters were plastered
throughout Italy showing Mussolini in a pose of triumphant
salute, superimposed on a map of Africa with Ethiopia indi-
cated as Italian. In the Dopolavoros, children's puppet shows
depicted Mussolini and Italian troops strewing the stage
with battle corpses of black-painted "African bandits and
barbarians."

King Emmanuel, now Emperor of Ethiopia by grace of
Mussolini's conquest, was required by protocol to award a
title to his Prime Minister. He called Mussolini to the
Quirinal and offered him the title of Prince, but Il Duce
was too shrewd to accept the bait, which would have bound
him closely to the royal family in a subordinate role.

"Your Majesty," he replied blandly, "I wish to remain
plain Mussolini, as I have always been."

Emmanuel looked upset. "But a peerage, at least?"

"The Mussolinis have always been peasants, and I am
rather proud of the fact." He placed his hands on his hips
in typical arrogance, and smiled grimly. "However, since
Your Majesty insists upon honoring me, I will accept
promotion from the rank of corporal in our armed forces."

"General?" the King cried hopefully.

"First Marshal of the Kingdom of Italy," Mussolini replied calmly. Emmanuel turned pale with anger. By tradition, that title belonged to one man only in the nation—the
King himself. He started to protest, but a fierce glare from his

pugnacious Prime Minister quickly forced him to swallow
his chagrin. Unable to trust his voice, he nodded his head.

Italy now had two First Marshals, and no one had any
doubt as to which one was all-powerful. Victor Emmanuel
never forgave Mussolini for this insult to the House of
Savoy.

Mussolini's real triumph in 1936 was political rather than
military. He had defied the League of Nations and had been
reprimanded by little more than a slap on the wrist—the
imposition of economic sanctions. And less than two months
after the fall of Addis Ababa, Anthony Eden, under orders
from London, led the move to lift the League's boycott.
Singlehandedly, Mussolini had broken the prestige of the
League and doomed it as a world force capable of keeping
the peace.

A new world crisis was shaping up in Spain, which in
July, 1936, had been a republic for five years. Two days
after the League called off sanctions against Italy, General
Francisco Franco led a military uprising against the Spanish
democracy. He disguised his raw grab for power on behalf
of Spain's wealthy classes with the camouflage which had
been so successful for Mussolini and Hitler—"saving the
nation from Communism."

Spanish workers and peasants rallied to the Loyalist government they had elected—a "Popular Front" coalition of
all shades of political opinion from middle-of-the-road to
extreme left. Millions of Spaniards became weekend soldiers,
working in fields and factories during the week, fighting in
the lines on Saturdays and Sundays.

Franco asked Mussolini and Hitler for help in swiftly
crushing the Loyalist government. Il Duce mulled over the
proposal with Ciano, Spain, he reflected, could be useful to
them as a testing ground for troops and equipment. Hitler

would undoubtedly reach the same conclusion. Mussolini determined to demand the use of Spanish naval bases in the Mediterranean as the price for helping Franco. That would give him a knife at both Gibraltar's back and France's belly. He wasn't worried that the West might aid the Spanish Loyalists. The democracies hadn't lifted a finger to save Ethiopia. He was convinced that the League was bankrupt as a world force and that a smart dictator could continue to bluff the democracies into backing off.

"Besides," he told Ciano with a sigh, "if Italians aren't kept fighting, the lazy pigs grow soft. Hitler's lucky. Germans are born Nazis. But Italians have to be *made* into Fascists!"

Foreign correspondents in Spain were aware that a new dimension had been added to the Civil War when, early in August, Italian crews in twenty-one Savoia-Marchetti bombers began to pound at Loyalist targets, and 50,000 Italian "volunteers" marched along with Franco's insurgents. Then a German Condor Legion air squadron showed up in Spain, and Hitler's tank corps were seen operating under cover of heavy Nazi artillery batteries. A frantic appeal from the Loyalist government to Russia brought limited assistance in the form of tanks and guns—only a trickle compared to Fascist armaments in Spain. The fighting grew bloody and savage. In the first two months of the war, 85,000 were killed, 300,000 wounded. Mussolini's bombers violated the Geneva Convention rules against attacking open cities. Revulsion against Italian pilots mounted so high that Franco advised Mussolini to recall his son Bruno from the Spanish National Air Force, explaining plaintively, "The enemy has begun to make special efforts to shoot him down."

Visitors to Italy between 1936 and 1938, kept abreast of the truth about Spain by an uncensored free press back home, were astonished at how completely brainwashed Italians were by grotesque lies they were fed in the Fascist press. In America, England and France, labor and liberals pleaded with their democratic governments to help Loyalist Spain, as Mussolini and Hitler were helping Franco. But the West, led by England, cautiously decided on a policy of "nonintervention." The Spanish War, said Britain's new Prime Minister, Neville Chamberlain, was "an internal matter," and all nations ought to keep hands off. Mussolini and Hitler gleefully joined twenty-seven nations of the League in signing a neutrality agreement, while Italian and German troops continued to fight for Franco as "volunteers."

In the United States, President Franklin D. Roosevelt grew increasingly critical of Chamberlain's appeasement policies, especially in the case of Spain, but a strong feeling of isolationism among Americans, most of whom wanted to keep aloof from Europe's quarrels, tied his hands. In May, 1937, Congress put into effect the Neutrality Act, forbidding the export of arms to foreign belligerents. In practice, it became a blockade against the Loyalist government, while permitting arms shipments to Mussolini and Hitler. German, Italian, British and French warships, meanwhile, jointly "policed" the Spanish coasts under the neutrality agreement, and all Loyalist aid was gradually choked off. Roosevelt called on the world to "quarantine the aggressors," but his plea fell on deaf ears.

Admiral Maugeri of the Italian Navy revealed in 1948 what the Spanish War had signified to the Fascists in 1936. "This," he said, "was the *real* beginning of the Second World War."

◆ 11 ◆

"BELIEVE! OBEY! FIGHT!"

"Pack my things, Rachele. I'm going to Berlin!"

It was September, 1937, and Hitler had invited Mussolini to Germany to sign the Anti-Comintern Pact, an alliance which bound together Germany, Italy and Japan. The pact was allegedly aimed against "international Communism" but was actually a smokescreen behind which the three enemies of democracy could swallow up other countries "to protect them from the Red threat." Japan was already using the pact as a shield behind which her troops were invading China. The Rome-Berlin axis, as Mussolini called it, was still rolling over Spanish Loyalist corpses.

Hitler met Mussolini personally and drove with him in an open car through mobbed boulevards. The crowds roared only, "Heil Hitler! Heil Hitler!" Il Duce turned slightly green at the German snub, Hitler's revenge for the Duce-shouting crowds of his Venice visit. To teach Mussolini which of them was the greater dictator, Hitler put on a huge display of Germany's mighty new weapons.

At a giant open-air rally in Berlin, the two dictators pledged their friendship before an immense mob that listened patiently despite a driving downpour. Hitler flattered Mussolini as a genius—"one of those rare geniuses who make history, and are not made by it!" Speaking in German, Mussolini announced, "Italian Fascism now has a friend

with whom it will march side by side to the end!" *Sig heil!
Sig heil! Sig heil!*

He returned from Berlin feeling depressed. Despite his
outward bravado, he had sustained a crushing blow to his
pride. The pupil had now far outstripped the master, and
the humiliating truth was that he was no longer in the
same league with Hitler. The Berlin dictator had built an
awesome war machine for world conquest. Mussolini strutted,
boasted, blustered—but he counted on bluffing his opponents
by a show of force. Italy's war strength was impressive only
against Ethiopian tribesmen or an amateur army like the
Spanish Loyalists.

Partly in fear of Hitler, partly in hope of ingratiating himself, the master began to imitate the pupil. He ordered
the Italian Army to learn a new marching step, the *passo
romano,* a German goosestep in disguise. He began to ful-
minate against "the world threat of Jewish Communism."
Drawing up a new law expelling all Jews from Italy who
had arrived in the past eighteen years, he sneered to King
Emmanuel, "About twenty thousand weak-minded Italians
will be sorry for the Jews."

"Count me one," Emmanuel said coldly, "I agree with
your former estimate of Hitler's anti-Semitism as idiotic."

Mussolini's eyes glittered. If this haughty little man did
not take care, he would wake up one morning uncrowned!

Italians were grumbling because the Spanish War seemed
to be dragging on endlessly, and hundreds of thousands of
Italian troops were still tied up in Ethiopia. Not only had
Ethiopia proved profitless, but the Spanish War had bled
the Italian economy white.

Mussolini anxiously sought to arouse a martial spirit like
Germany's with stirring sings and posters: *Fight the Red
Beast Everywhere! . . . Remember the Atrocities of Red*

Aviators in Spain! . . . Everything for the State—Nothing Outside It, Nothing Against It! . . . Our Rome—We build for It, We Conquer for It, We Die for It! His masterpiece was a three-word command painted in huge black letters on every pier, building wall and mountain cliff throughout Italy: *Credere! Obbedire Combattere! . . . Believe! Obey! Fight!*

He ordered Squadristi throughout Italian cities to beat up anyone suspected of grumbling over the war, listening to foreign broadcasts or telling anti-Fascist jokes. "A few heads and many radio sets have been broken," he reported grimly to the Grand Council of Ministers.

Admiral Maugeri said later, "Honest Italians were shocked, disgusted, outraged. Our attitude toward Fascism changed. For a while, though revolted by his Squadristi and their murderous methods, a certain sympathy persisted for Mussolini personally. He was a sick man, we told ourselves. . . . Despite excruciating stomach pains, he worked and slaved, day and night, dedicating himself unremittingly to the Italian people—or so we thought in our innocence."

In December Mussolini told Ciano that he was going to take Italy out of the League of Nations. "It's toothless and useless now, anyhow. And it will prove to Hitler that he can depend upon me."

Ciano, who had usually played the sycophant to his father-in-law, even to the point of aping the strut and out-thrust jaw in public, now felt sure enough of himself to risk voicing his doubts. "Duce, it's dangerous to trust Hitler—"

"I know he's unbalanced in many ways."

"Worse. He's treacherous. He'll use us to help him swallow the other countries. Then he'll turn and swallow *us!*"

Mussolini looked uncomfortable. "Don't you think I recognize the risk? Listen, Galeazzo, we have no choice. We simply don't have anything like the strength of Germany. Our only real protection against German invasion, let alone building a world empire, lies in being Germany's ally!"

It was a confession of weakness he dared make to no one else, the real secret why he felt compelled to lash Italy to Germany's chariot in the mad plunge toward war.

Hitler, meanwhile, was stirring up a storm of fear in the West with threats of annexing Austria and "the German Sudetenland" of Czechoslovakia. London and Paris tried to appease him by secret assurances they would look the other way if he would use "evolutionary means" to gain his ends— that is, pressure and internal overthrow. Hitler called Austrian Chancellor Schuschnigg to Berlin and ordered him to turn over control of Austria to the Nazis of Vienna. Schuschnigg rushed to see Mussolini, whom he considered a personal friend and ally.

"I had the feeling of sitting opposite a maniac," Schuschnigg told him. "How can I turn my people over to such a man! I'm going to refuse. I'll order a plebiscite on March thirteenth, and let Austrians vote whether they want to remain independent or be absorbed by Germany."

"Hitler will never stand for it," Mussolini said.

Hitler didn't. Two days before the plebiscite, jackbooted Nazis stormed across the Austro-German border. Hitler dashed off a message to Mussolini, explaining that anschluss (political union) by force was necessary because Schuschnigg had been unreasonable. "Please have no concern for Italy's security," he assured Il Duce. "I have drawn a definite boundary between Italy and us. It is the Brenner. We will be good neighbors."

"Hitler might at least have let me know in advance,"

Mussolini grumbled to Ciano. "Well, there's no help for it now. It's a fait accompli. London and Paris have protested, but that's all they're going to do. Send Hitler our greetings and tell him Austria doesn't interest us at all."

Hitler was more than a little relieved, because Mussolini's anger might have bent or broken the Rome-Berlin axis.

"Tell Mussolini I will never forget this!" he fervently assured the diplomat who brought the message from Rome. "Never, never, never, whatever happens! If he should ever need any help or be in any danger, he can be convinced that I shall stick to him, whatever may happen, even if the whole world be against him!"

It was one of the rare promises that Hitler kept.

Italians were shocked by the anschluss, but even more shaken by their leader's permitting the "German barbarians" to drive south to Italy's very borders. The Western press criticized Mussolini for failing to live up to his pledge that he would protect Austrian independence. On March 16, 1938, he made an indignant speech denying that he had ever made such a pledge, either verbally or in writing. Even if the outside world scoffed, at least no one *inside* Italy would dare stand up and call Il Duce a barefaced liar!

Mussolini invited Hitler back to Italy early in May. "It might not be a bad idea," he told Ciano, "to make him aware that the Italian people are strong enough to defend Latin civilization. Just in case he gets any ideas!"

Ciano nodded. "We'll impress him with our naval power in Venice, our armies in Rome and our culture in Florence!"

Hitler was met at Rome's railroad station not by Mussolini, but by King Emmanuel himself, acting as host, who took him to the Quirinal as a royal guest. Indignant, Mussolini remained aloof during the pageantry in Rome and Naples, and finally took Hitler off to Florence to speak to him alone.

The Fuehrer was in a jubilant mood. He told Mussolini that Spain and the anschluss proved that the West wouldn't fight. The democracies were old and tired. If they played their cards right now, they could soon divide France between them, and the world would fall into their hands, piece by piece.

Mussolini looked worried. "You really think England and America would let France go under? They didn't in the World War."

"There were no strong dictators in the last war!" Hitler's lip curled. "Who are the leaders who frighten you? Daladier —a dime-a-dozen French politician? Roosevelt—a cripple in a wheelchair? Chamberlain—a doddering old man afraid of his shadow?"

Mussolini knew that Hitler despised Prime Minister Neville Chamberlain most of all as the architect of Britain's appeasement policy. Chamberlain felt that Germany had legitimate grievances because of the harsh penalties imposed upon her by the Versailles Treaty and that if these grievances were met Germany would be reasonable and calm down, pacifying the turbulence in Europe.

In the months that followed, Mussolini watched uneasily as his volatile partner massed two huge armies of Panzers and motorized troops like a nutcracker around the vulnerable neck of Czechoslovakia, also sending five divisions to the French border. French Prime Minister M. Edouard countered by rushing reinforcements to the Maginot Line, France's gigantic system of fortifications protecting her eastern border.

In September Hitler thundered his dreaded demand that the Sudetenland of Czechoslovakia must be ceded promptly to Germany, or his juggernaut would roll. In near-panic,

Chamberlain flew twice from London to appeal to Hitler to negotiate his demands. The Fuehrer scornfully refused, shouting that unless his ultimatum was met at once, he would march in four hours.

Chamberlain sped an urgent request to Mussolini to act as peacemaker between the Axis and the West. Delighted at this unexpected turn of events, Mussolini kept the phone lines hot with calls to Hitler, Daladier and Chamberlain as the time bomb of war ticked ominously away. With less than an hour to go before the Germans were scheduled to invade Czechoslovakia, he succeeded in arranging a meeting in Munich between Hitler, Chamberlain, Daladier and himself.

Hitler was in high spirits at the Munich Conference, obviously delighted at having both England and France nervously seeking to placate him. Mussolini acted as interpreter for the quartet, since he was the only one who spoke all four languages. For the first time Hitler looked at his junior partner with genuine admiration, even meekly taking his cue from Mussolini as to when to laugh, nod or say no.

Il Duce sensed that although Chamberlain and Daladier were prepared to sacrifice the Sudetenland to Hitler, they had to save face before the world. He proposed a "compromise" whereby Hitler would agree not to go to war and would instead be allowed to occupy the Sudeten territory in stages over a period of ten days. The Western diplomats quickly agreed, and Hitler nodded amiably. The conference ended on a further ironic note when the quartet sat down to sign the agreement and found no ink in the inkwell. Hitler flew into such a tantrum at this inefficiency that Mussolini was secretly alarmed he might call off the whole pact.

Chamberlain used the occasion to sign a separate treaty with Hitler, each promising to confer on all future problems that concerned their two countries, "to assure the peace of Europe." Chamberlain returned to London announcing triumphantly, if naïvely, "It is peace for our time."

Mussolini returned to Venice and the wild cheers of mobs who hailed him as "peacemaker of the world" and "angel of peace" as he drove beneath a giant triumphal arch of laurel leaves. His expression grew grimmer and grimmer. Fools! Whose stupid idea was it to glorify him as a peacemaker, instead of as a clever diplomat? Didn't the idiots realize what Munich *really* meant?

Mussolini began to feel his years when his sons Vittorio and Bruno married and moved out of the Villa Torlonia. Now that the three oldest children were no longer there to amuse him during his visits, he saw less and less of Rachele, and more and more of Claretta Petacci. She was flattered when he kept the world's ambassadors and ministers cooling their heels in the anteroom, even ignoring calls from Hitler and Chamberlain, in order to enjoy her company.

There was increasing resentment over his attachment to La Petacci. Italians who were discontented over high taxes, high prices and low wages found her a convenient scapegoat for their troubles. Why, it was costing the government over eight million lire a year to keep her in that special flat in the Palazzo Venezia! And soon after Claretta had taken up quarters in the Palazzo Venezia, her brother Marcello had become rich on black market operations based on inside information; her sister Miriam had been given a contract as a movie "star"; Claretta herself was showered with ex-

travagant gifts by industrialists who sought fat government
contracts through her favor.

When Chamberlain came to Rome in January, 1939, he
carried over his arm the same umbrella he had taken on his
trips to Germany, and which had become a world symbol
for appeasement of Fascism. During his conference with
Mussolini in the Palazzo Venezia, the umbrella was mislaid,
setting in motion a frantic search. When the story got around,
Rome roared with laughter. "Now Mussolini has talked him
out of his umbrella, too!"

The British Prime Minister had come to insist on assurances from Mussolini that he would restrain Hitler from
any further warlike moves. Angered, Il Duce kept him
standing while he sat majestically in the only chair allowed
in his office, his own, delivering a blistering attack on England for the sanctions imposed by the League on Italy
during the Ethiopian venture. Afterward, Mussolini told
Ciano scornfully, "These English are no longer the Drakes,
Nelsons, Rhodes, Raleighs and Kitcheners who built their
empire. Now they're just the soft sons of the wealthy who
deserve to lose that empire—and will!"

In the early spring of 1939, Italian and German might
triumphed in Spain, and Franco took power. By this time
Hitler was positive he could nibble democracy to death
piece by piece without serious opposition. Accordingly, on
March 15 he advanced from the Sudetenland to occupy
Prague, the capital of Czechoslovakia. More or less as an
afterthought he notified Mussolini in a dispatch.

"Every time Hitler occupies a country," Il Duce fumed to
Ciano in a rage, "he sends me a message! What a partnership!" Ciano suggested that they teach Hitler a lesson by

occupying Albania and then informing Berlin. So they did. Hitler only laughed at the gesture.

On May 22 Hitler decided the time had come to sign a "Pact of Steel" with Mussolini, pledging them both for ten years to fight as allies in any war. It was a warning to the West that the Rome-Berlin axis could not be split and that war with one would mean war with both. Mussolini hoped that Hitler would now feel obligated to notify him beforehand of any dangerous war moves he planned and that Italy would then be able to restrain Germany until Il Duce felt ready.

The pact created great uneasiness throughout Italy, but many Italians consoled themselves with the cynical reflection that Mussolini was a great realist, and would respect the pact only so long as it suited his purposes. But they, as well as the rest of the world, were stunned when only three months later Hitler suddenly signed a nonaggression pact with the one nation he and Mussolini had persistently told the world was the greatest menace to civilization—the Soviet Union. The West was astonished as this cynical development. Those who had criticized Chamberlain's appeasement policy as knuckling under to Fascism had been assured that if Hitler were allowed to expand eastward, he and Stalin would collide head on in Poland, and what was wrong with letting the two dictators destroy each other? But the nonaggression pact between Moscow and Berlin made it plain that there would be no Russo-German war and that instead Poland would be amicably carved up between the two giants.

"This means war," Mussolini told Ciano thoughtfully. "Hitler has protected himself by locking the back door. Now he's ready to turn and take on the West!"

King Emmanuel was greatly agitated. He, too, understood

that war with England and France was now only days away, and he was fearful of the consequences to Italy if she were dragged to the battlefield tied to Hitler's war chariot because of the Pact of Steel. He called Mussolini to the Quirinal, and the two men quarreled bitterly.

"The pact was a ridiculous mistake!" Emmanuel fumed. "Our industry is wholly dependent on coal from England. All the British have to do is seal off Gibraltar and Suez, and where will we get the raw materials we need? You should have made a pact with Chamberlain—not with Hitler!"

"I intend to curb the Fuehrer's impetuosity by explaining Italy's situation," Mussolini replied frostily. "When he understands, he will not move against the West until we are ready. But *we* might as well have an understanding right now as to which First Marshal of the Empire is going to direct that war when it comes."

"Mussolini, I warn you—"

"No, Emmanuel, I warn *you!* In Italy the war will be conducted as it was in Africa, by one man alone—myself! If you have any different ideas, you may possibly go down in history as the last King to reign in Italy!"

• 12 •

TIGER BY THE TAIL

As the Nazi tiger crashed through the boundaries of
Europe, Mussolini grew more and more apprehensive about
clinging to its tail. He couldn't make up his mind which
would be more dangerous—to hold on or let go. His indecision mounted agonizingly as crisis led to crisis through
1938 and 1939.

He knew that with the giant Skoda arms factories of
Czechoslovakia in Hitler's hands, an attack on Poland would
soon follow. Mussolini did not have long to wait. In August,
Hitler began screaming to the world about the "terrible
atrocities" committed against Germans living in the Polish
Corridor. This was the strip of Poland that cut off East
Prussia from Germany and contained the Baltic port of
Danzig, largely inhabited by Germans but important to
Poland, and neutralized under the League of Nations as a
"free city."

In March, 1398, Chamberlain attempted to stiffen Polish
resistance to Hitler's threats by promising that both Britain
and France would come to Poland's aid if the Nazis invaded
and the Poles fought. Mussolini promptly summoned the
British ambassador to Rome and warned that if England
sent troops to help Poland, Italy would take up arms at Germany's side.

But only two weeks later a worried Duce cautioned Hitler

that Italy couldn't possibly be ready for war for at least three more years and urged that a peace conference be held now instead. "You can get everything you want in Poland without going to war," he wrote, "whereas war with Poland would certainly turn into a general war." Hitler's own General Staff tried to convince him that Mussolini was right.

"If it comes to war, it will only be a short war, and it will be won by Germany!" Hitler screamed, "If there is war, I shall build U-boats, U-boats, U-boats! I shall build planes, planes, planes, and I shall annihilate my enemies!"

Mussolini sent Ciano to meet Germany's Foreign Minister, Joachim von Ribbentrop, at the latter's estate in Salzburg. On August 11, during dinner, Ciano asked bluntly, "What do the Germans want, Ribbentrop? The Polish Corridor? Danzig?"

"Neither. What we want is war."

Shocked, Ciano asked to see Hitler the next day. "Frankly, Fuehrer," he told the fanatical little dictator, "we are greatly surprised at Germany's willingness to risk total war, in view of Il Duce's explanation that Italy will be in no position to fight one until 1942."

"Tell my dear friend, your great leader, that he need have no anxiety about Poland. I'm personally convinced that the Western democracies will back down again, as usual."

Two days before the announced date for invading Poland, Hitler was grimly warned by Chamberlain, who now recognized the folly of appeasement, that England would fight for Polish independence. Mussolini became frightened and decided the time had come to let go of the tail of the tiger. He rushed word to Hitler to count on Italian support only if the Nazi attack on Poland did *not* bring on war with England or France.

"I consider it my bounden duty as a loyal friend to tell

you the whole truth and inform you beforehand about the real situation," Mussolini informed Hitler prudently. "Not to do so might have unpleasant consequences for us all."

Hitler raged around his chancellery all through the afternoon of August 25, uncertain whether to defy England, furious at his Axis partner's decision in face of peril. Mussolini, meanwhile, suffered pangs of humiliation, fully aware of the shameful figure he was cutting by running out on the Pact of Steel. Desperate to put a better face on his timidity, he rushed another note to Hitler promising to enter the war on Germany's side—*if* the Fuehrer would make it possible by supplying Italy with a year's war necessities, adding up to 170 tons and requiring 40,000 trains. The list enclosed, Ciano observed cynically, was "enough to kill a bull—if a bull could read it."

Hitler held up the attack on Poland to think things over. He restrained his impulse to denounce Mussolini as a cowardly jackal and sent word instead that he understood Italy's position, but would appreciate it if Mussolini kept his intentions secret from England and France. Il Duce hastily promised, then brooded for days over whether he was making the correct decision. If the democracies backed down, as they always did, he would have lost a chance to share in Hitler's spoils. On the other hand, if the democracies forced Hitler to back down, he might blame Mussolini and attack Italy.

On August 31 Hitler mobilized his divisions on the border of Poland. At 8:00 P.M. that evening Ciano made an alarming discovery. The British had cut off all telephone communications with Rome. He ran to Mussolini's office. "Quickly, Duce," he gasped. "There's not a moment to lose! The Allies are getting ready to attack us. They think we're with Hitler in the Polish affair!" Mussolini immediately sped a message to Chamberlain: "Decision of the Italian government is taken. Italy will *not* fight against either England or France."

As dawn broke on September 1, 1939, Luftwaffe squadrons roared into the Polish sky from Germany, and forty-four Nazi divisions swept across the frontier, spearing toward Warsaw in three gigantic arrows. Two days later Britain and France declared war on Germany, honoring the pledge to Poland. World War II had begun.

Watching these shattering events grimly from Washington, President Roosevelt hinted at their future significance to Americans by declaring an unlimited national emergency on September 8. This was the first step of a plan agreed upon by Roosevelt and the United States Joint Planning Committee on Armed Forces to prepare Americans for the defense of the Western Hemisphere against Fascist aggression, by becoming the "arsenal of democracy" if Britain and France were forced to fight Hitler.

The world received another shock two weeks later when Soviet armies attacked Poland from the east, and the fate of that unhappy nation was sealed. As Hitler and Stalin carved up the prize between them, Mussolini watched fretfully, constantly debating with himself. He felt that England couldn't stand up against the German war machine. Even if the Americans decided to come in, they were too far off and couldn't build up a big enough war effort to turn the tide before Hitler won. On the other hand, he was gloomily aware that conflict between Italy and Germany was inevitable. He felt this in his blood and kept asking himself whether an English victory wouldn't be more desirable for Italy's future than victory by Hitler.

He clung shakily to a policy he called "nonbelligerence," which he preferred to the word "neutrality." There was some small comfort in finding himself being wooed by both America and Germany, each seeking to influence his position in the world conflict. Roosevelt had sent a special envoy, Sumner Welles, to try to persuade Mussolini to renounce the Rome-Berlin axis. Welles was shocked at the sight of the fifty-six-year-old Mussolini, whom recent events seemed to have aged into a slow-moving, heavy, tired-looking man with a worry-lined face. The American diplomat gave him Roosevelt's warmest greetings and suggested that F.D.R. would enjoy meeting him personally in the Azores. Flattered, Mussolini promised to think it over.

Three days later London announced that the British Navy was stopping any ship carrying German coal from Rotterdam to Naples. Mussolini was furious. "How *dare* they!" he stormed to Ciano. "Do the democracies expect me to stay neutral if they treat me like this?"

Hitler rushed Ribbentrop to Rome to take advantage of Il Duce's anger at England. The Nazi Foreign Minister promised Italy a million tons of coal a month, delivered by rail, and warned Mussolini not to be lured by any blandishments from America. Did Il Duce realize that Roosevelt, Morgan and Rockefeller were part of "an international Jewish banker plot against the Fascists and Nazis?"

Mussolini and Ciano exchanged glances of derision, but Il Duce's anger against England, and his gratitude for Hitler's offer of the coal Italy badly needed, combined to push him closer to Berlin. To Ribbentrop's delight, Mussolini said, "Tell the Fuehrer I agree that my place is at his side on the firing line. The question is not *whether* Italy will enter the war on Germany's side, but only *when*. I cannot at this time, however, set any exact date. Events will determine that."

Ribbentrop rushed back to Berlin jubilantly. Hitler

listened grimly to his report, then snapped, "Events will not determine that date—*I* will! Phone Ciano and set up a meeting between Mussolini and myself in six days."

The two dictators met in Il Duce's private railroad car at the Brenner Pass on March 18, 1940, as thick wet snow out of the Alps pelted the train's windows. Mussolini, nervous at having finally committed himself, hoped that Hitler would be grateful enough to make the meeting simply a friendly get-together to denounce the democracies, but Hitler had no intention of listening to any more empty oratory. He ranted and raged at Mussolini, permitting no interruption of his torrent of words. Mussolini sagged lower and lower in his seat, helplessly fascinated and dominated by Hitler's supreme self-confidence.

Mussolini could not delay entering the war much longer, Hitler railed. Did he want Italy left out in the cold as a second-class power? Out of Hitler's loyalty to their friendship, he would make Italy's share of the war an easy one. Mussolini could stay out until Hitler's drive against the French and British armies in northern France. Then Italy would only have to turn their rear with an attack from the northern Swiss frontier. Mussolini meekly promised that Hitler could count on him to attack as soon as Germany advanced victoriously into France. Alarmed that he might have gone too far, he added hastily that he meant at the strategic moment, of course—when the Allies were staggering, so that a second blow could bring them to their knees. Hitler shrugged contemptuously, and the meeting ended.

As the German armies went from victory to victory, the pressure on Mussolini to join them grew increasingly greater. Hitler sent him films of Nazi military operations in Poland, Norway, Denmark and the Netherlands. When Mussolini screened them at the Villa Torlonia, he sighed. "What a steel hurricane those Nazis are!" And now they were on his doorstep. If he didn't add Italy's contribution in blood to theirs, Hitler alone would dictate the future of Europe, and that would be the end of Latin civilization. Italy would cut a poor enough figure coming into the war this late, but at least it would give them a claim to *some* of the cake.

When King Leopold of Belgium surrendered on May 28, Mussolini told Ciano grimly, "We're already dishonored enough. Any more delay is out of the question. We have no more time to lose!" He sent for General Badoglio and Balbo.

"I'm notifying Hitler we will be ready to declare war on England by June fifth," he told them, hands on his hips, chin thrust forward like Il Duce of old.

Badoglio was aghast. "Impossible! We're totally unprepared for a major war effort. We haven't a fraction of the arms, tanks and planes we'd need. We don't even have enough shirts for our soldiers. It would be suicide!"

"The war will be over by September. I need only a few thousand dead to sit at the peace conference as a belligerent."

Word flashed around the world that Italy was mobilizing. Roosevelt sent a personal message to Mussolini on May 30, pleading with him to stay out of the war. Two days later King Emmanuel sent for Ciano. "There is no enthusiasm among our people for this war," the monarch warned. "Those who talk of a short and easy war are fools. This is not 1915!"

Ciano nodded forlornly. Mussolini had forgotten Machiavelli's warning that it was fatal to shoot at tigers unless you killed them. "I'll try one last time to dissuade him, Excellency."

He pleaded with his father-in-law, "Why fool ourselves? Our people have no stomach for real war, Hitler's war—"

"I'll get them to gallop into it!" Mussolini roared. "All the cowards need is beating, beating and *more* beating!"

On June 10, 1940, he took the Italian people for a ride on the back of the tiger.

Italians were shocked and dismayed at suddenly finding themselves fighting allies of the Germans they feared and detested. Mussolini's propaganda machine swiftly whipped up ancient Italian hostilities toward France, promising that victory would be sweetened by a revenge that would unfurl the Italian flag over the French territories of Corsica, Savoy, Nice and Tunisia. "If I'd have been successful," he explained three years later, "not one person in Italy would have questioned the morality of it. In politics there is no morality—there is only success or failure. Nothing else. History seizes you by the throat. You have not time to debate issues or weigh moral values. You must act—and act at once!"

Mussolini was convinced that his intervention had been in the nick of time and that he had shrewdly purchased shares in an inevitable victory. Hitler's mighty war juggernaut was splintering opposition everywhere as though it were so much glass. He had overrun Poland in three weeks. Denmark had fallen in two hours, Norway in two months. Holland and Belgium had succumbed in six weeks. Twelve days later the German armies smashed through French defense so decisively that France surrendered unconditionally at Compiegne, on June 22, 1940.

In contrast, Italy's own campaigns went badly right from the start, as the King, Ciano and Badoglio had warned. Mussolini swept aside his professional generals and admirals and directed the whole Italian war effort himself, although he had never risen higher than the rank of corporal during World War I. "Hitler was a corporal, too," he declared defiantly. "For that matter, so was Napoleon—the Little Corporal who was the greatest military genius the world has ever known!"

Far from being a genius of the battlefield, Mussolini made one terrible blunder after another. If a general dared dispute his strategy, Il Duce drew himself up with the grandeur of an ancient Caesar and thundered, "You argue with the conqueror of Ethiopia, the architect of victory in Spain?" When his orders proved calamitous, he roared at his generals and admirals, calling them nitwits, incompetents, blockheads, cowards.

On August 13, Marshal Rodolfo Graziani invaded Egypt with ten Italian divisions. Trying to follow Mussolini's orders from Rome, Graziani stumbled from disaster to disaster. The British mounted a counteroffensive under General Archibald Wavell that, with a crack desert force twelve times as small, routed Graziani's whole army in sixty-two days, knocking it out of the war and taking 130,000 relieved Italian prisoners.

Graziani, whose military experience had been largely limited to horrible massacres of the Ethiopians, was as much to blame as Mussolini. A captured Italian colonel charged bitterly, "The high command is trying to fight this campaign out here as a colonial war. Can't the fools see that this is a modern European war and must be fought by modern European methods? They think just because this is Africa they should use methods suitable for fighting savages!"

Mussolini felt humiliated when Hitler suddenly sent troops into Romania without bothering to notify him. "Hitler's trying to freeze us out of the Balkans," Ciano warned darkly. "Why don't we put a spoke in his wheel by invading Greece without telling *him*?"

Mussolini was delighted with this idea because it would divert attention from Graziani's humiliating mistakes in Africa. On October 28 Italian forces abruptly attacked Greece from Albania. Hitler was furious when he heard about it, because late fall was the worst time of the year to start a campaign in the Balkans. He feared that the invasion would only bring British troops and planes to Greece, putting the whole Balkan position in danger. Hitler was right. Less than a week after the invasion, the fierce Greeks had beaten the Italians back across the border and, more ignominious still, were chasing them through Albania. Aghast, Mussolini rushed to the Albanian front to try to stiffen Italian backbones.

While his car rolled to an observation post, he heard someone call out to him in the dialect of the Romagna, "Don't go up there, Duce! They mean to kill you!" He looked thoughtful, but continued on to the observation post, where he watched a battle through a telescope on a tripod. A sense of uneasiness drove him to leave fifteen minutes ahead of time. Two minutes later a shell struck the post.

When Mussolini returned to Rome he was freshly suspicious of everyone around him, suspecting conspiracy. He had dark doubts especially about the King, Badoglio and now even Ciano. After all, hadn't the whole miserable fiasco in Greece been Ciano's idea? As the Italians continued to retreat through Albania, Mussolini fastened the blame on Badoglio, but his Chief of Staff told the Fascist Grand Council, "The real trouble lies entirely in Il Duce's command of the war." Mussolini denounced the aged Marshal as a "traitorous enemy of the regime," and Badoglio indignantly resigned. After an agonized night of wrestling with his pride, Il Duce dispatched a humble plea for help to Hitler. The disgusted Fuehrer sent troops to his rescue, and in a few weeks the Germans had nailed down victory in Greece.

Meanwhile, in November, 1940, Hitler leashed the full might of his Luftwaffe against England in the hope of blitzing the tough little island into ruins and submission.

But the British, inspired by their new leader, Winston Churchill, stood up valiantly under the terrible bombings. In March, 1941, the Roosevelt Administration succeeded in persuading Congress to pass the Lend-Lease Act, enabling the United States to abandon its position of neutrality and rush huge amounts of food and military supplies to England. This new development frightened Mussolini, who dreaded America's entry into the war. Meanwhile, humiliation continued to follow humiliation for the unlucky twentieth-century Caesar.

In the spring of 1941 a handful of daring British units, plus columns of tribesmen from the hills, swept the Italians out of Ethiopia. On May 5 Emperor Haile Selassie rode triumphantly back into his capital of Addis Ababa, delighted with the new roads, hospitals and schools the Italians had built during the five years of his exile.

Threatened with complete disaster in North Africa, Mussolini again had to humble himself by another appeal to Berlin. Hitler rushed three of his best armored divisions, led by General Erwin Rommel, to retake the territory lost by Graziani to the British. Ribbentrop groaned to Hitler, "The greatest stroke of genius the Allies ever had was to antagonize Mussolini into joining *our* side!"

Mussolini seemed to shrink physically as the hard truths of war deflated his legend and his bluster. He grew more and more envious of Hitler's triumphs and resentful of the open contempt with which the German dictator now dealt with Rome. He was tired of acting as Hitler's taillight, and felt that it would have been a blessing to Italy—and the world—if the recent assassination attempt on Hitler had succeeded.

The deeper Mussolini's fortunes sank, the more angrily he refused to listen to unpleasant news from commanders in the field, the more he shouted down advice. Soon the only minister who dared to tell him the truth was Ciano. Relations between the two men became cool and strained as a result, and Mussolini became increasingly convinced that Ciano was secretly plotting behind his back to succeed him as dictator.

"Your husband is too ambitious," he muttered to his daughter Edda. "He loves pomp too much, and he's greedy for power. Warn him to care as much for Italy as he does for himself!"

Personal worries and grief weighed as heavily upon him these days as the misfortunes of war. One night in March, 1941, he was awakened by a phone call that brought news of Edda, who was serving as a Red Cross nurse on the Italian hospital ship *Po*. The ship had been mistakenly bombed at night by British planes, and many aboard were drowned or missing. Mussolini paced the floor in an agony of suspense until another call came through hours later, reporting that Edda had been in the sea for five hours, numb with cold, but had finally been rescued at dawn and would be all right. When he put down the receiver, it was wet with perspiration.

Less than four months later, at 8:05 A.M. on August 7, Bruno Mussolini took off in his plane from the airfield at Pisa. The engines suddenly cut out, and the plane plunged to earth. The last words the control tower heard were, "Dad . . . the field!"

Mussolini was shaken by a grief so intractable he fell into a deep melancholy. He was haunted by the fact that the son born during the first World War had died during the second. Was there some mysterious meaning in Bruno's birth and death? Was it a mystic sacrifice of blood the ancient gods of Rome had demanded of Il Duce for his devotion to war?

He withdrew even further from human contacts, wrapped in gloomy thoughts, spending most of his time alone except for afternoon visits with Claretta and summer holidays at Riccione with Rachele and the children. On his orders the lights of his office study were kept burning late every night, to give the impression to those who looked up that Il Duce was working long hours to keep the Italian ship of state afloat.

• 13 •

RETREAT FROM GLORY

A midnight phone call on June 22, 1941, woke Rachele at the Rocca delle Camminate, the old castle in the Romagna near Predappio which Mussolini used as a summer estate. "Please inform Il Duce at once, signora," said the crisp voice of the German military attaché in Rome, "that Germany has declared war on Russia!"

Rachele hurriedly woke her husband and told him. "What?" He groaned. "Hitler's mad, mad! Stalin would never have dared to attack us. But now we will have to fight on two fronts!"

He rushed to Salzburg to find out why Hitler had decided to double-cross Stalin two years after the signing of their nonaggression pact. Hitler told him that with France knocked out of the war, England would need another sword in Europe. Who else could that sword be but Russia? Churchill would pay any price Stalin demanded, but, Hitler boasted, he was foiling Churchill by attacking Stalin before Stalin attacked him. He was confident it would take him only a few months to liquidate Russia and capture all the food, minerals and slave labor he needed. Mussolini expressed doubts that the Soviet Union would collapse that quickly. Hitler confided that he knew the whole Soviet plan of mobilization and defense, which his spies had bought in Moscow five months before. He was positive that the plan was authentic because his agents had just learned that the Russians who had sold it to them had be caught and executed.

Hitler's brash attack on Russia astonished the democracies, who greeted the development as a stroke of luck for their side. Much of their anger at Stalin for his pact with Hitler dissolved in their pleasure at having another powerful nation in their camp. Hopeful voices in the West began to recall that Napoleon's great mistake had been invading Russia; they hoped it would be Hitler's, too.

But Hitler's armies swept through the Ukraine, meeting little effective resistance as they arrowed toward Moscow and Leningrad. Mussolini hastily joined the "blitz" by sending an Italian Expeditionary Force. The German armies were halted only by the cruel Russian winter, just when the Soviet Union appeared on the verge of collapse. "The enemy in the East has been struck down and will never rise again!" Hitler broadcast jubilantly to the world as his armies reached the gates of Moscow on December 5.

Two days later Japan launched a surprise attack on Pearl Harbor, and the next day the United States declared war on Tokyo. Mussolini and Hitler jointly declared war on the United States on December 11, inspiring Roosevelt's fiery denunciation of Italy for her stab in the back. An American declaration of war on Germany and Italy followed a few hours later.

Mussolini hurled back a crude personal insult. "Never in the course of history," he sneered, "has a nation been guided by a paralytic! There have been bald rulers, fat rulers, handsome, even stupid rulers—but never rulers who had to be carried to the dinner table by other men!"

Il Duce hoped that Hitler was right, that "America was a big bluff" entering the war too late to help the Western powers. Hitler certainly had reasons for his optimism. The

American Navy had been rendered powerless by Japan; Russia was almost defeated; the British were staggering back toward Egypt under the relentless blows of Rommel's Afrika Korps. Italian tank divisions in the desert, stiffened by German officers, were now fighting twice as hard and successfully as they had under Graziani.

Rommel made little attempt to disguise his scorn for the Italians under his command. He had fired Graziani as Italian Commander in Chief in North Africa, and also refused to allow Italian fighter pilots to escort German bombers because "they are more likely to shoot *us* down than the enemy fighters they're aiming at." When the German high command wired they were sending Rommel reinforcements consisting of 20,000 Italian infantrymen, the "Desert Fox" snapped back, "I asked for soldiers, not ditchdiggers!" Rommel's insults did not escape Mussolini's ears, nor did reports from Germany that Italian laborers working there were being treated as slaves, beaten for insubordination and laziness, and guarded by vicious watchdogs.

A great hatred for the Germans was being stored in his heart, Il Duce confided bitterly to Ciano. "In the end I will square accounts, no matter how long it takes!" The barbarian Huns would pay for their insults to a race which had given Caesar, Dante and Michelangelo to humanity.

On June 21 Rommel captured Tobruk, key to British defenses in the Middle East, and two days later the Afrika Korps clanked across the Egyptian frontier. The British were swept out of El Alamein, seventy miles from Alexandria at the head of the Nile. Staring across the hot sands at the Pyramids, Rommel called a temporary halt to await the new supplies he needed to conquer Egypt and the rest of the Middle East.

Mussolini had asked Marshal Ugo Cavallero, successor to Badoglio as his Chief of Staff, to notify him when the Italian Army began the advance under Rommel that would take them to the Suez Canal. Il Duce planned to lead Italy's tanks in the victory parade through Cairo. When Cavallero told him the time had come, Mussolini flew to the Italian sector in Libya. He later called the date of his arrival, June 28, 1942, the turning point of both the war and his own personal fortunes. For three weeks he waited impatiently for Rommel to advance, enduring constant complaints from Italian commanders.

He wearily promised that the Italian troops sent to Africa would be better-trained and that badly needed supplies would reach the Afrika Korps once Malta was pulverized by the German Air Force. The British Navy, operating from that island base in the Mediterranean, had been sinking over a third of all reinforcements and supplies the Axis shipped to Libya. The British Broadcasting Corporation had punned satirically, "The American Navy drinks whisky and the British Navy prefers rum, but the Italian Navy sticks to port!" Another BBC joke referred to Mount Vesuvius as a "British lighthouse" because it couldn't be blacked out, and lit up the Italian ships in the Bay of Naples as targets for British bombers.

Hitler had given Rommel the order to attack Cairo, but Rommel argued that he just didn't have the equipment and fresh troops he needed to advance. Disgusted with waiting, Mussolini returned to Rome, desperately tired and ill.

The battle for Stalingrad began in August, 1942, with Stalin mustering over a million fresh troops to throw against the German Sixth Army. Hitler's Chief of General Staff, General Franz Halder, urged him to pull back the Sixth

Army to the River Don for a strong defense. Hitler refused, screaming that he wouldn't leave the Volga, and fired Halder for protesting.

From that time on Hitler no longer heeded his General Staff and made all his own military decisions. The Stalingrad battle raged until the end of January, when all that was left of Hitler's Sixth Army—90,000 Germans—surrendered to Russian Marshal Rokossowski. The Soviet armies began a gigantic counteroffensive to sweep the Nazis out of Russia, and for the first time in World War II the initiative passed to the Allies.

"Those treacherous Russians!" Hitler moaned to Mussolini when the two dictators met. The plans his spies had bought in Moscow had been fakes. What could he do with a barbarian government that even killed two of its own operatives to convince him that they were really traitors and so mislead him in his strategy?

Mussolini sighed and shook his head. "It's the 'law of contrariety,' Fuehrer. There are times when everything in life goes exactly the opposite from the way you plan it!"

Il Duce's new theory, the "law of contrariety," seemed to be operating on the African front also. Rommel, with no reserves of men, tanks or oil, wearily radioed Hitler for permission to withdraw his battle-worn troops to safer positions forty miles west. Instead, Hitler again ordered him to attack Cairo, raging, "You can show your troops no other way than that which leads to victory or to death!" Rommel knew now that he was dealing with an absolute madman. Attacked at El Alamein on October 23 by British General Bernard Montgomery, the Desert Fox led the Afrika Korps in a swift, brilliant withdrawal that frustrated Montgomery's attempts to trap him.

As the British pursued Rommel across the burning sands

all the way to Tripoli, the Italian mayors of town after town welcomed them as deliverers rather than conquerors. "After suffering under the Germans," one mayor sighed, "to be your prisoners is heaven, gentlemen!"

The ailing Mussolini received a fresh shock on November 8, when General Dwight D. Eisenhower suddenly landed in French North Africa at the head of an Anglo-American expedition of 300,000 troops. It was now obvious that the Allies planned to squeeze and destroy the Afrika Korps in the vise forged by the converging armies of Eisenhower and Montgomery. Rommel's retreat to Tripoli brought new humiliation to Mussolini because of the spectacle offered by entire Italian divisions surrendering to the nearest American or British corporal.

"We were eager to get out of that miserable war we never wanted in the first place," one Italian colonel explained to an American intelligence officer. "And we hated the Germans with all our hearts. In the retreat from El Alamein they seized all the transport, ours as well as theirs, leaving us to fight our way back on foot, short of food, water and ammunition!"

Things were going far from well on the Italian mainland. Soon after the Axis began suffering reverses in Africa, Allied planes began to strike at the industrial cities of the North. Workers fled from Allied bombing raids in panic. Smashed railroads crippled the economy. Peasants in the South began to suffer from hunger and lack of medical supplies. Eggs in the cities sold for a quarter each, and shoes, when obtainable, for up to eighty dollars a pair. There were mass strikes in Milan and Turin for "bread, peace and freedom." Millions of Italians listened to forbidden BBC broadcasts for war news they could trust. Mussolini became glumly aware that his people were rapidly coming to the end of their endurance.

Regiments went overseas uncheered and unnoticed, except for audible sneers of "more meat for Mussolini!"

Il Duce raged to Ciano, "This second-rate Italian race are good for nothing except singing and eating ice cream! They completely lack character. They're not serious enough. Too individualistic, too cynical, too concerned only with pleasure! One bomb falls on a work of art, and they weep to the heavens! I'm *pleased* when the Allies bomb our cities. It will toughen this race of cowards who don't deserve me!"

At the same time he shared his people's soaring aversion for the Germans. The time was coming, he felt bitterly, when he would have to fight them. They were taking everything and leaving Italy with nothing. It was a thorn in his heart that by helping Hitler he had lost an empire.

He kept bombarding the Fuehrer with messages urging him to come to terms with Russia in order to turn the full might of the Axis against the West. When Hitler coldly refused, Mussolini then suggested calling a secret meeting with Churchill to reach an agreement that would free them to use all their strength against Russia alone. "I know how to talk to Churchill," he bragged to Hitler. "I know him intimately." Again his partner turned a deaf ear.

Early in January, 1943, Mussolini relieved Ciano as Foreign Minister and sent him to the Vatican as Ambassador to try to get the Pope's help in negotiating a separate peace with the Allies. What neither he nor Ciano knew was that the British had already received another message from Rome, *via* Switzerland, offering the Allies the cooperation of Marshal Badoglio in overthrowing Il Duce. But on January 26 both these backstage plots came to naught when Churchill and Roosevelt met at Casablanca and announced firmly that the only peace terms offered the Axis would be "unconditional surrender." Badoglio's offer to lead a revolt against

Mussolini was rejected as premature. The Allies felt that at this point in the war Il Duce was an albatross around Hitler's neck, actually helpful to the West by forcing German divisions to stay pinned in and around Italy in case the Allies invaded or Italy defected.

Mussolini's painful illness continued all through the winter and early spring of 1943. Agitation, exhaustion and bitterness brought on constant ulcer attacks that often sent him writhing to the floor in agony and left him looking haggard and worn. Finding it impossible to sit still, he turned, twisted and fidgeted convulsively in his chair, sometimes biting his fist to keep from crying out. Reports of each new war disaster plunged him into a bitter mood that made him lash out at anyone close by.

Feeling he had to escape from Rome, he phoned Rachele at the Rocca and told her, "I've decided to join you and see if I can get better up there." But his private demons pursued him to the Romagna, and he became increasingly unstable, flying into wild rages at the slightest excuse. There was little doubt that he was having a nervous breakdown.

Morale sank to rock bottom in Italy as Tripoli fell to the Eighth Army on January 23. Somebody had to pay for the loss of Libya, Mussolini decided. On February 6 he announced the "discovery" of a plot to sabotage the war effort and overthrow him as dictator. Out of the Cabinet went Cavallero, his bungling Chief of Staff, and a handful of other Fascist ministers he considered expendable, including Dino Grandi, who had been with him for twenty-four years.

If no real conspiracy had existed, one began now, centered around General Vittorio Ambrosio, who succeeded Cavallero as Chief of Staff. A deep-dyed Royalist, Ambrosio won King Emmanuel's consent to a plot which would end the Fascist regime in Italy and overthrow Mussolini. "Roosevelt and Churchill will never sit down at the same table with Il Duce," Ambrosio told Emmanuel. "Our only hope is to set up a democratic government under you, Sire, and led by Badoglio."

If Mussolini was having trouble with his generals, so was his Axis partner. "My generals do not tell me the truth!" Hitler raged to Joseph Goebbels, his propaganda chief, in March. "They are all dishonest, all enemies of National Socialism! I get ill when I think of them!"

Hearing of the high-level plotting going on in Italy against Mussolini, and learning of Il Duce's painful illness, Hitler felt a rare moment of compassion. He sent for Mussolini, insisting that the Italian leader must be treated by his own private physician. Mussolini flew to Salzburg on April 7, taking along his own doctor and his own diet food. At the last moment, however, his physician persuaded him not to trust a German doctor, so Hitler used the occasion to build up his Italian partner's faltering morale.

"The Duce underwent a complete change," Goebbels reported later. "When he got out of the train on his arrival, the Fuehrer thought he looked like a broken old man. When he left four days later he was in high fettle, ready for any deed." Hitler had told Mussolini that Germany had developed a secret weapon that would win the war—the V-2 rocket "buzz bomb" that would fly over the English Channel and destroy London and other English cities, one by one. Mussolini returned to Rome with a new feeling of omnipotence. "All I have to do," he boasted, "is appear on the balcony and all of Rome will rush to listen and cheer! My enemies say I'm finished. We'll see . . . when I send them all to prison camps!"

Suddenly and without warning, the full impact of war hit

the Italian people. Allied bombers from advanced North African air bases began to raid the city of Naples. Italian curses against Mussolini became more bitter, frequent and open in the South of Italy. He ordered the siren sounded in Rome every time Naples was pounded from the air. "It will toughen the Romans and make them realize there's a war on!" he growled. But the citizens of Rome, wearying of false alarms, learned to ignore the sirens. When Allied bombers finally did blast Rome, the casualties among civilians were dreadful.

On May 8, 1943, the Allies entered Tunis in triumph, and the defeat of the Axis in Africa was complete. Mussolini began to spend sleepless nights, knowing that the invasion of Sicily and Italy's mainland was now only weeks away. Ordering blackouts of all Italian cities, he retired again to the Rocca, where he tried to forget his troubles cutting wood, scything grass and playing solitaire.

Rachele now organized her own system of spies to keep tabs on new plots in Rome against her husband. She was shocked to discover that one conspiracy was being led by her son-in-law Ciano. When she warned her husband, he scoffed, "Oh, those informers of yours! You're always suspicious of Galeazzo because he enjoys hobnobbing with aristocrats at the Albergo Ambasciatori!"

On the seventh anniversary of Italy's conquest of Ethiopia and proclamation of empire, Mussolini appeared on the balcony of the Palazzo Venezia to speak once more to the crowds in the square below. Rousing himself to a pitch of enthusiasm that for a moment made Italians see him as the dynamic Il Duce of old, he shouted, "I feel your voices vibrating with unshakable faith! Have no fear—ultimate victory is ours! All of your sacrifices will be rewarded! That is as true as it is true God is just and Italy is immortal!"

The crowd, carried away by its hunger to believe him, cheered enthusiastically. But it was to be Mussolini's last balcony speech.

Shortly after dawn on July 10, he burst into his wife's room. "Rachele, Rachele, wake up! The Americans and British have landed in Sicily!" On June 11 the Allies had struck north from Africa to the tiny island of Pantelleria, halfway between Tunis and Sicily. Now they had leap-frogged again to Sicily, in preparation for an invasion of the mainland of Italy itself.

Mussolini cursed savagely, beating his fists against his temples. "That miserable Guzzoni I sent to hold the island hasn't fired a shot for the honor of Italy! Even the promise of a marshal's baton hasn't kept him from bolting for the hills like a frightened cur!" He groaned in agony, "Oh Rachele, who is there left for me to trust? I am alone, alone, alone!"

• 14 •

OVERTHROW OF A DICTATOR

On July 19 Mussolini was summoned to Feltre by Hitler, who was deeply worried as the Russians advanced on his east and the Anglo-American forces surged north from Africa. During their three-hour conference, Hitler raged, screamed, pounded the table. What kind of dictator was Mussolini to let the Allies grab Sicily without a shot fired by the Italian divisions there? All Italian forces must be placed under German command at once. Italy down to the Po Valley must be turned over to Field Marshal Albert Kesselring.

"I—I'll talk it over with the Grand Council," Il Duce stammered miserably. They were suddenly interrupted by his secretary, who brought them news that Rome was under heavy air attack at that very moment—the Allies' first raid on the Eternal City. Stunned, Mussolini rose from his chair and paced the conference room in a fever of anxiety.

"Rome" he said tragically. "They *dare* to bomb Rome!"

Scorn edged Hitler's voice. "What did you expect? Did *you* hesitate to bomb Madrid, Barcelona or Addis Ababa?"

The bombing of Rome was a devastating blow to the Italians, who had never quite believed that the Allies would hit at the birthplace of the world's first republic. When five hundred Allied bombers, mostly American, blew up Rome's railway freight yards, war factories and airfields, thousands fled the city, touching off demonstrations for peace in all parts of Italy.

Allied bombers were already pounding Italy's industrial centers daily, sowing confusion, crippling food distribution, smashing factories, wiping out roads. Mussolini's advisers carefully kept from him the news that his name was now being cursed openly on the nation's streets.

Italians in high places were well aware that Il Duce's days in power were now numbered. Two major conspiracies had been organized to overthrow him—one Fascist, one Royalist. The Fascist plotters were headed by Count Dino Grandi, Mussolini's Minister of Justice, and included Ciano and Farinacci. The Royalist plotters were the King, Badoglio, Ambrosio.

Rachele Mussolini, always suspicious of the men around her husband, uncovered evidence of both conspiracies and tried to warn him. "Rachele," he replied in exasperation, "I'm worrying about American tanks in Sicily, not about petty intrigues. *They* go on all the time!"

At the request of Grandi and other Fascist leaders, a meeting of the Grand Council was set for July 24 in the Palazzo Venezia to hear Mussolini's report on his Feltre conference with Hitler. Rachele was deeply worried. "They mean to destroy you!" she warned. "Arrest them all now before the council meeting opens—before it's too late!"

"Nonsense!" he scoffed. "How can you imagine that these cringing underlings I've dominated for twenty-one years would dare defy me?"

At 5:15 P.M. he strode into the great hall opposite the Sala del Mappamondo and took his place on a thronelike chair at the head of a huge U-shaped table. The twenty-eight blackshirted ministers of the Grand Council rose, gave him the Fascist salute and barked, *"A noi!* To us!" This pledge of loyalty was prudently hedged by a revolver in every pocket, as well as a couple of hand grenades in Grandi's briefcase.

Looking tired and gray with illness, Mussolini made the opening speech. "At this moment I am easily the most disliked, indeed most hated, man in Italy," he admitted. "Yes, the war is unpopular. But what war was ever popular? This war was Mussolini's war, and I take full responsibility for it! But am I to be blamed for the mistakes of others? At Feltre even Hitler heaped coals of fire on my head for the poor fighting spirit of our troops, the cowardice of our generals, the whining of our civilians under bombardment!"

Yet when he finished, it was apparent from the flinty glances around the U-shaped table that the old Mussolini magic to beguile his followers had lost its potency. Grandi rose to deliver a cold, blunt attack upon the founder of Fascism.

"Duce," he accused, "you lost the devotion of the people the day you tied Italy to Germany! You brought us into this cursed war against the honor, feeling and interests of the nation. We have already lost one hundred thousand dead, and one hundred thousand Italian mothers are crying out, "Mussolini has killed our sons!"

Il Duce jumped up and roared "That's a lie!"

But Grandi coolly ignored him and continued his blistering attack. He finished by proposing that the council end Mussolini's dictatorship and restore the government of Italy as a democracy under King Emmanuel. Il Duce was so stunned by this defiance that he slumped back, muttering in disbelief, "My luck's turned—it's turned!"

Ciano rose in support of Grandi, but tried to soften his disloyalty by throwing the blame on "German treachery." His father-in-law stared at him with cold fury and snapped contemptuously, "I know well enough where treachery lies!"

Mussolini made one desperate attempt to stampede the council into voting against Grandi's proposal. "I might remind you of the private fortunes most of you have built up through graft!" He tapped his briefcase ominously. "I have enough proof here to send most of you to the gallows. You, Ciano, more than anyone! If you lose me you'll also lose the war—and your precious skins!"

"Blackmail!" shouted Grandi.

Mussolini called for a vote. Nineteen voted with Grandi, eight against and one abstained. Mussolini jumped to his feet. "You have provoked a crisis!" he shouted. "The meeting is closed!" When a loyal follower tried to end the council session with the usual salute to him, he snapped bitterly, "No! No! I free you from that!"

Stunned by his defeat, he left the room followed by a dwindling coterie of supporters who urged him to jail the other ministers. But he felt too ill and tired to do anything and returned home. "You were right," he admitted to Rachele.

"Arrest the traitors!" she urged him frantically.

"My orders don't count anymore," he sighed. But to pacify her he ordered the arrests of Grandi and Ciano. Word came back that they had fled to the Villa Savoia, putting themselves under the protection of the throne. Then Victor Emmanuel summoned Mussolini to the palace, and Royal aides emphasized that Il Duce was to appear in civilian clothes, not in uniform.

"That will make it easier to arrest you!" Rachele fretted. "You mustn't go! Don't trust the King!"

"Nonsense!" he scoffed. "What would Italy be without Il Duce? All they mean to do is to relieve me of the military command. Frankly, I'll be happy to be rid of it!"

Closeted with the King in his study, Mussolini took the initiative by fuming against the Grand Council for voting against him. "Your Majesty must agree to the arrest of these traitors for treason to the head of the government."

"*I* am the head of the state," Victor Emmanuel corrected him coldly. "It's no use, Mussolini. It's all over. Not only is the council against you, but you've also lost the confidence of the Italian people. At this moment you are the most hated man in Italy. You have only one friend left—me. You needn't worry about your personal safety. I shall see to that. I accept your resignation as head of the government, and I shall charge Marshal Badoglio to form a new caretaker cabinet."

The color drained from Mussolini's face, and he seemed to shrink and grow older before the monarch's eyes. "Then it's all over," he whispered incredulously, wavering as though on the verge of fainting. "The end of Fascism!"

Leaving the Villa Savoia, he brooded that his biggest mistake had been made in 1922 when he marched his triumphant Blackshirts in front of the Quirinal Palace instead of through it. Now he bitterly regretted his peasant awe of the King that led him to spare Emmanuel only to be repudiated in his hour of crisis. As he was looking around for his car, he was approached by a captain of the carabinieri, who saluted.

"The King has commanded me to protect you from the mob, Duce. This way, please." The police officer led him to a Red Cross ambulance. Mussolini climbed in beside six carabinieri armed with machine-pistols, and the ambulance screeched off at top speed for police barracks. Even then it did not occur to him that he was under arrest and that the twenty-one-year-old Fascist dictatorship of Italy was actually over.

The cry swept through Rome: "They've arrested Mussolini!" Despite the blackout, crowds surged through the streets in wild celebration. The same people who had once enthusiastically roared the name of Il Duce now smashed statues of him, threw portraits of him into the street and tried to set fire to Fascist headquarters. They had made terrible sacrifices for him, believing as he told them, "Il Duce is always right!" Now, after twenty-one years, they had to face the bitter truth that their sacrifices had been in vain. Yelling curses at the fallen leader, they cheered the King, danced in the great squares of Rome and sang, "The war will soon be over now!"

Listening to the public rejoicing from his barracks imprisonment, Mussolini wrote bitterly in his journal, "What can we say of a people that makes a spectacle of itself before the rest of the world, by such a sudden and almost hysterical change of heart?" His humiliation was deepened by the fact that not a gun had been fired, not a voice had been raised, to protest his being cast down from the heights.

The generals and administrators who had deserted him rushed to join the new government. Badoglio immediately opened secret negotiations with the Allies for Italy's surrender; at the same time he sent solemn assurances to Hitler that "the war goes on for us in the spirit of alliance." Badoglio knew it was now only a matter of time before Hitler would decide to occupy Italy. His only hope was to stall the Fuehrer until he could arrange for the Allies to pour their armies into Italy.

Hitler's Chief of Operations, General Alfred Jodl, was the first to break the news to him of Mussolini's downfall.

"Only a general would believe such nonsense!" Hitler scoffed. "Dictators *can't* be overthrown!" When Jodl's news was confirmed, the Fuehrer flew into a wild rage over the

treachery of royalty and gave orders that all German princes
were to be thrown out of the Wehrmacht, or Regular Army.
When he received Badoglio's promise to keep Italy in the
war, he sneered to Jodl, "More Royalist deception! Pretend
to believe him, but keep feeding our divisions into Italy!"

Mussolini, meanwhile, was brooding over his fate. Would
Badoglio turn him over to the Allies as a war criminal? Was
he marked for an assassin's bullet?

Badoglio wrote him a letter keeping up the pretense that
he was being held in custody only to "protect you from plots
against your life." Mussolini penned a humble reply express-
ing gratitude, promising not to oppose him in any way, and
offering to retire to the Rocca della Caminate with his
family. But inwardly he seethed with resentment and dark
despair. Was this to be the sum total of his reward for
serving his country in war and peace for twenty-one stormy
years?

Then one night, he was spirited out of the police barracks and was driven to a pier ironically named Ciano Wharf.
Here he was saluted by Rear Admiral Franco Maugeri, Chief
of Naval Intelligence, and taken aboard the corvette
Persefone.

Maugeri was shocked at the great change that had taken
place in his celebrated prisoner's appearance. Il Duce's face
was thin and sallow, his cheeks sunken. "His huge, hypnotic,
snakelike eyes shone out of the darkness startlingly," Maugeri
recalled later. "The celebrated outthrust chin didn't look
very strong now. Only three days before, this crumpled
figure had been the supreme power in the land. Though I
hated him for everything he stood for and had done, for the
crimes he had commited against humanity and civilization,
for having betrayed Italy and sold our people into slavery—
still I could not help feeling a little sorry for him now."

Il Duce turned petulant aboard the *Persefone*. "Why must I be persecuted in this way?" he whined at Maugeri. "Since last Sunday I've been completely cut off from everyone. I've had no news of my family. I'm without a penny. All the clothes I have are the ones I'm wearing. Why should I be treated this way—like a common criminal?" Once he grumbled, "What are they scared of, anyway? I've been completely betrayed. I'm all through politically!"

But neither Hitler nor Badoglio was through with him. Badoglio needed him as a sacrificial goat to offer the Allies, while Hitler needed him as window dressing for the German invasion and control of Italy. Aware that Badoglio was keeping Il Duce carefully hidden, Hitler summoned a daredevil SS officer, Captain Otto Skorzeny, for a dramatic secret mission.

"I cannot and will not leave Mussolini to this fate," he told Skorzeny grimly. "He has got to be rescued before these traitors can surrender him to the enemy. I have selected you to find and save my friend!" The plot was named "Operation Student" after German General Karl Student, who was readying paratroops to overthrow the Badoglio government.

Meanwhile the *Persefone* put in at the tiny island of Ponza, west of Naples. Mussolini knew Ponza well—he had used it as a place of banishment for his own political enemies. Two of them were still on the island—Zaniboni, the Freemason who had been the first to attempt to assassinate him eighteen years earlier; and Socialist Pietro Nenni, his former comrade who had gone to jail with him in Forli during his pacifist days. Neither Zaniboni nor Nenni approached Mussolini during his ten days on the island, and he spent all his time translating Italian poems into German.

On July 29, 1943, his sixtieth birthday, Badoglio forwarded a telegram of congratulations from Goering, which Mussolini correctly interpreted as a hint that Hitler had not forgotten him and was planning a rescue. Badoglio also suspected as much because he sent Maugeri back to Ponza to whisk Mussolini away to a new hiding place—a guarded villa in La Maddalena, an empty little isle at the northern tip of Sardinia.

"The Germans aren't the only danger," Maugeri admitted to his prisoner en route. "If the British knew where you were, they'd try to land Commandos by submarine to capture you."

On La Maddalena Mussolini ate alone, listened to the radio, read the papers and studied a set of Nietzsche's works that Hitler had sent him for his birthday. He wrote a letter to Rachele, telling her, "You are worthy of a different man from me. I have always caused you bitterness and trouble. Will you send me some warm clothing, as I have only what I went to see the King in? Also the boots I am wearing are already badly worn, and I'd like to have a pair with stronger soles."

A German reconnaissance plane was seen flying close to the island on August 26, and Mussolini was again rushed to a new hiding place—this time to the Gran Sasso Hospice, a winter sports hotel at Campo Imperatore, 6,500 feet up in the Italian Apennines. Staring around at the machine-gun pits guarding the empty hotel, Mussolini sighed, "Well, this time they've got me in the *highest* prison in the world!"

One day, walking around under escort and admiring the rugged, craggy peaks hemming in the ten-mile plateau of Imperatore, he called a greeting to a shepherd grazing his flocks in the valley below. Recognizing him, the shepherd replied coldly, "You've got us all into a lot of trouble, and now you're in it, too!" However, another shepherd managed to get close enough to him to whisper, "The Germans are at the gates of Rome, Excellency. They're looking everywhere for you—I'll tell them you're here." He kissed Mussolini's hand and added, "When I tell my wife I've seen you, she won't believe it!"

Mussolini was so touched that he almost wept. Only that morning he had noted gloomily in his diary, "If I had any friends, now would be the time for them to sympathize, literally to suffer with me. But since I have none, my misfortunes remain within the closed circle of my own life."

He listened each day as radio news told of Allied air raids destroying whole areas of Naples, Turin, Milan and Genoa. Then on September 3 came the announcement that the American Fifth Army had landed south of Naples at Salerno, and five days later the report that Italy had surrendered. Badoglio had signed an armistice with the Allies, and he and the King had fled from Rome to Pescara. Tuning in Berlin, Mussolini heard Hitler raging at Badoglio for agreeing, as part of the armistice, to deliver up to the Allies "the greatest son of Italian soil since the collapse of the Roman Empire!" Mussolini trembled with angry passion. He was convinced the Allies wanted to exhibit him in a cage in Madison Square Garden in New York, like a wild animal; he vowed they would never take him alive.

On the afternoon of September 12 he suddenly saw ten gliders soaring out of the clouds directly toward Imperatore's plateau. The lead glider landed with a shuddering crash two hundred yards from the hotel. German troops leaped out, some with machine guns, some with carbines, and rushed toward the hotel. Other glider troops followed.

Two carabinieri in front of the hotel gaped in stupefaction, unable to believe or react to what was happening. An alarm sounded, and other armed Italian police came running out. Lieutenant Faiola rushed into Mussolini's room, pistol in hand, and shouted, "Shut the window and stay where you are!" But Il Duce ignored him, having noticed an Italian uniform among the German troops.

"Can't you see an Italian general?" he shouted out the window. "Don't shoot! Everything's all right!" The confused carabinieri held their fire as the Germans dashed into the hotel yelling, "Duce! Duce! Duce!" Otto Skorzeny cleared a path to the stairs and raced up three steps at a time. Encountering the colonel in charge, he demanded immediate surrender. The Italian commander shrugged, ordered red wine and offered Skorzeny a glass.

"To the victor," he bowed with Gallic aplomb. Italian General Soleti, who had accompanied Skorzeny from Rome as a hostage, joined the two men in the toast. When Skorzeny was taken to Mussolini's room, the German commando stared in surprise at the bearded ailing man he had risked his life to rescue.

"Duce, I have been sent by the Fuehrer to free you!"

"I knew my friend Adolf Hitler would not abandon me!" Choked with emotion, Mussolini embraced Skorzeny.

A tiny German Storch spotter plane landed on the plateau. The pilot argued with Skorzeny that it would be impossible to take off with three men aboard. Skorzeny replied grimly, "It's a gamble. But if we return without Il Duce—that's certain death for both of us. You know the Fuehrer never forgives failures!"

The three men squeezed into the fragile little aircraft, which raced desperately off the edge of the ravine. One of its wheels hit a rock, and it plunged downward toward the valley floor. A bare hundred feet from crashing, the pilot slowly brought its nose up and sent it soaring above the jagged peaks.

Pale but jubilant, Mussolini shouted in relief. He was intoxicated by the sheer melodrama of his escape—a fitting climax to sixty years of melodrama. "I knew it!" he cried jubilantly in German to Skorzeny. "My blood told me we couldn't crash. It's my destiny to end my days only when I'm once more raised to the heights I've always occupied—high above the mob!"

It was an accurate prophecy.

• 15 •

ESCAPE TO DISASTER

Mussolini's rescue and escape set all Europe ablaze with excitement. Speaking to Parliament, Prime Minister Churchill compared it to the flight of a captive Caesar and admitted, "The stroke was one of great daring."

Mussolini was reunited with his family in Munich. Rachele told him that Edda and Ciano, with their three children, were being held by the Germans in a villa near Munich. Ciano wanted a passport for Spain, but the Germans had a score to settle with him for his attempts to sabotage the Rome-Berlin axis. Goebbels had labeled him a "poisonous toadstool" and "the evil spirit of Fascism."

On September 14 Mussolini was flown to the Fuehrer's headquarters in East Prussia. Hitler was shocked to see the formerly proud, arrogant Il Duce now transformed into a pitiful shell of a man, old, worn, tired beyond caring, no longer a Caesar.

"What do you intend to do now?" he demanded.

Mussolini shrugged moodily. "I suppose I had better retire. To fight Badoglio now would only bring on civil war."

"Nonsense!" the Fuehrer snapped. "What kind of a dictator are you, anyway? You must have revenge on those in the Grand Council who betrayed you and went over to Badoglio. They must be tried and shot!"

"But my role is finished. . . ." Il Duce quavered.

"No! It is your duty to continue fighting at my side! I have already set up a new Italian Fascist government in northern Italy. You will take it over."

Mussolini sighed. "But why go on? How can we win now?"

"We *will* win, I tell you!" Hitler screamed. "London will be smashed by my flying bombs. And in a year I shall have atom bombs so terrible the Allies will surrender at once before I wipe them off the face of the earth!"

Mussolini squirmed in an agony of indecision. "Give me a few days to think it over—"

"I'll give you six hours! Just remember that a snap of my fingers can wipe out millions of Italians, just as I wiped out millions of Jews, Czechs, Poles and Russians!"

After Mussolini left, Hitler expressed only contempt for him, but he admitted to Goebbels that he could not allow him to retire. That would make it evident to the world that Mussolini no longer believed in Fascist victory. If he refused to return to Italy as Hitler's puppet, Goebbels was to arrange for his death in an "accidental" air crash.

When Mussolini gloomily reported his interview with Hitler to Rachele, she urged him not to accept. He had fought enough and was entitled to retire in peace.

"Hitler's mad," he said. "He'll destroy Italy if I refuse. There's no help for it—I'll have to go on carrying my burden to the end!"

On September 18 he broadcast over the Munich radio appealing to the Italian people to support his new Fascist Socialist Republic: "Descendants of Caesar, Dante, Leonardo! Rays of their glory shine proudly on all Italians. But so, too, are we shamed by the recent deeds of dishonorable Italians. To wipe out this disgrace we must be prepared to face the trial of trials—trial by blood. Italians, follow me!"

But his low, weary voice had lost its magic. Goebbels told Hitler scornfully, "A waste of breath. Even Mussolini can't make anything out of Italians—but Italians!"

If the Italian people were reluctant to fight for Fascism, however, they were not slow to fight against it. An underground army of partisans now waged guerrilla warfare against Marshal Kesselring's German troops in Italy. As the Allies fought their way up the Italian boot across blown bridges and blasted roads, villagers rushed out of their half-destroyed cottages weeping with joy and pressing gifts of wine, flowers and chickens upon their deliverers. The famous American author John Steinbeck accompanied the advance as a war correspondent. "Whatever may have been true about the Fascist government," he reported, "it is instantly obvious that the Italian little people were never our enemies."

Mussolini set up headquarters of the new Fascist Socialist Republic at Salo on the shore of Lake Garda. To show Hitler that he was, indeed, still a strong man imbued with the old Romagna spirit of vendetta, he arranged a swift trial of all former ministers of the Fascist Grand Council who had not escaped from the country.

"You must not try Galeazzo!" Edda Ciano stormed at her father. She begged him to forgive her husband for the sake of her children.

He replied testily, "Roman patriots never hesitated for a moment to sacrifice their own children. Here I am neither father nor grandfather—only Il Duce of Fascism." He hesitated a moment, then tried to make her understand. "Besides, Hitler wants Ciano to die!"

"If your court murders my husband," she cried hysterically, "I'll reveal secrets that will shock the whole world!"

He grew angry. "You're on the verge of a nervous break-down, Edda. Place yourself in a nursing home!"

The special court at Verona condemned Ciano to be exe-cuted, along with General De Bono, Marinelli and two other ministers.

Mussolini was aware that the SS guards and spies sur-rounding him were not there just to "protect" him. He regarded General Karl Wolff, head of the Nazi SS in Italy, as his jailer, and worried about what Hitler would do if he failed to recruit a new Fascist army under Marshal Graziani. To add to his woes, Claretta Petacci and her family settled down in a nearby villa.

When Rachele became aware of Claretta's presence, she upbraided her husband. He swore that he had not sum-moned Claretta, and would in fact send her away. But each time he pleaded with Claretta to leave him in peace, she cried and begged him to let her share his fate. Bitterly aware of how little loyalty he had found when his fortunes had soured, Mussolini could not find it in his heart to spurn her.

Rachele finally took matters into her own hands and con-fronted Claretta. She ordered her to leave immediately, "for the sake of Italy." There was a stormy scene. Then Claretta phoned Mussolini and begged him to tell her what to do. He informed her sadly that Rachele was right. They must not see each other again. Claretta promptly fainted, and Rachele swept out in triumph.

The month of June, 1944, brought fresh reverses to the Axis cause. General Eisenhower's forces invaded northern France on D-Day, June 6, and General Mark Clark's Fifth Army took Rome, first Axis capital to fall to the Allies. Mussolini promised his supporters, "Don't worry—Rome

ESCAPE TO DISASTER   179

is my passion. We shall march to Rome and remain there
forever! Rome has possessed me ever since my young days.
On October twenty-eighth I shall address you from the
balcony of the Palazzo Venezia!"

On July 20 a group of high-ranking German officers attempted to kill Hitler in a bomb plot, but succeeded only
in paralyzing his right arm and puncturing his eardrums.
Mussolini, en route to Rastenburg by train for a conference,
was met by a pale, shaken Hitler who told him what had
happened.

"Fuehrer," Mussolini assured him solemnly, "your mir-
aculous escape is a sign from heaven!"

"Yes!" Hitler shrieked. "It shows I am the Man of Destiny
chosen to save Europe and the world! One thing is certain
—democracy can never replace Nazism or Fascism in Europe.
I know I can count on you, Duce. Believe me, you are the
finest, perhaps the only friend I have in the world!" Mussolini shook his hand warmly. "Perhaps now, Fuehrer, you
can understand that Il Duce is not the *only* dictator who
has traitors at his back!"

All through the summer and fall of 1944 Italian partisans
kept attacking both German troops and Blackshirts, and were
massacred in turn. In northern Italy a state of virtual civil
war existed. Mussolini was horrified by the reprisals which
Kesselring was taking against Italian hostages—killing ten
civilians for every Nazi soldier killed by an Italian partisan's
bullet. "The Germans have no sense of fairness at all!" he
lamented.

He turned gloomier, more thoughtful and abstracted.
Urged by his indignant staff to stand up to the Germans,
he replied, "The game is lost. Who would want to cooperate
with me? The conquered have no friends. The truth is that
we can do nothing against Hitler—we are his slaves!"

He had a brief flurry of hope in December when he visited Milan and was cheered by 40,000 people who shouted, as in the golden days of Fascism, *"Duce! Duce! Duce!"* The Milanese, shocked by the brutality of the German troops occupying their city, hoped that Mussolini's visit meant liberation from Nazi tyranny. "In twenty years of Fascism," he told Rachele dazedly, "I have never had such a welcome!"

On April 18, 1945, he moved his headquarters from Gargnano to Milan, but just one week later he was forced to flee north again to escape partisan units spearing into the city at the head of advancing Allied armies. Leading a convoy out of Milan in uniform with a machine gun over his shoulder, he admitted wretchedly to one of his ministers, "The agony is atrociously long. I'm like the captain of a ship in a storm. The ship has been wrecked, and I'm in the furious ocean on a raft which it's impossible to steer!" Bursting mortar shells and wild crackling gunfire drowned out the end of his lament.

"Where are we headed?" the minister shouted.

"Who knows? Possibly to Switzerland—possibly to death!"

They stopped in Como for the night. Here, with thirty cars full of officials, Mussolini waited for the 5,000 troops who were to accompany him across the border to join German forces in Bavaria. Brooding in a hotel room overlooking beautiful Lake Como, he felt stirred to write a farewell letter to Rachele.

"Here I am at the last stages of my life, the last page of my book. We two may never meet again. That is why I am sending you this letter. I ask your forgiveness for all the harm I have unwittingly done you. But you know that you are the only woman I have ever really loved. . . . Take the children with you and try to get to the Swiss frontier. There you can build up a new life. I do not think they will refuse to let you in, for I have always been helpful to them and you have had nothing to do with politics. Should they refuse, surrender to the Allies, who may be more generous than the Italians. Take care of Anna and Romano, especially Anna who needs it so badly. You know how I love them. Bruno in heaven will help you. My dearest love to you and the children. Your Benito. Como, 27th April, 1945, Year XXII of the Fascist Era."

Instead of the 5,000 Italian troops he had been told to expect at Como, a single armored car joined him. It was driven by Alessandro Pavolini, his Minister of Popular Culture, and had in it only a dozen soldiers. "This is all," Pavolini apologized miserably. "The rats are deserting the sinking ship!"

Many of the supporters who had accompanied him from Milan were now hiding out in Como, waiting for an opportunity to surrender to the Committee for National Liberation, the militia of the partisans. Mussolini did gain one new carful of supporters willing to follow him into exile in Germany—Claretta Petacci and her family. Although he had arranged for their escape to Spain by plane, she was determined to stay at his side out of devotion which would not be shaken even by his previous rebuff. He was touched by her loyalty, and permitted her to join the convoy.

North of Menaggio they joined a motorized German column heading for the Swiss border. Mussolini learned that the Italian partisans now had control of the area and were stopping all vehicles to inspect them for Fascists trying to escape, allowing only the Germans to pass on. His personal guard, Fritz Birzer, an SS Lieutenant, insisted he must change into a German overcoat and helmet. He let himself be disguised, transferred to one of the German lorries, and sat next to the driver. An hour later partisan troops stopped the convoy and arrested all the Italians in it, including Claretta. The German lorries were waved ahead.

At the border town of Dongo the convoy was halted again for a final inspection. Mussolini turned up his coat collar and pushed his helmet over his dark sunglasses. Slumping deep in his seat, a Bren gun between his knees, he pretended to be asleep. The partisan inspecting the column stared at him.

"Drunk," the German lorry driver explained.

But the partisan was suspicious. He summoned his superior, Urbano Lazzaro, who confronted Il Duce. "Aren't you an Italian?"

Mussolini hesitated only a moment. What was the use of prolonging the inevitable? Humiliated by his disguise, he wished now only to regain some tattered shreds of his lost dignity. He raised his head tragically. "Yes," he said, "I am an Italian."

"Excellency!" Lazzaro was so startled that the old term of respect came out involunatrily. "So you *are* here!"

He was taken to a nearby frontier post in the mountains and held prisoner in a barracks room. Despite the cold he took off his overcoat and threw it on the floor, putting on instead some blue overalls he found in a corner of the room.

"I never want to see a German uniform again," he growled to the partisan guarding him. When a fire was lit for him and a meal brought, he seemed to recover his spirits and became almost cheerful, as though finding peace in defeat. He had only been asleep a few hours when he was awakened and driven south in a rainstorm toward a little village five miles north of Como. En route a fresh surprise awaited Mussolini. His car was joined by a second one carrying Claretta Petacci. Hearing of his arrest, she had begged the young partisan commander of Dongo to let her share his fate. They embraced wordlessly, and were driven to a farmhouse where they were sheltered for the rest of the night.

The morning dawned clear and beautiful, the air pungent with the smell of wet grass. It was April 28, 1945. On that day Adolf Hitler was marrying his mistress, Eva Braun, in an underground bunker in Berlin, just before both committed suicide. It was six days before the German armies began surrendering; sixteen days after Franklin D. Roosevelt had died in office and Harry S. Truman became the new President of the United States.

At 4:00 P.M. a partisan colonel, Walter Audisio, confronted Mussolini with a Bren gun under his arm. "Hurry up," he said abruptly. "I've come to set you free."

"Really?" Il Duce's brows rose sarcastically as he eyed the weapon. "How very kind of you!" He exchanged glances with Claretta and saw that she was not deceived either.

They were taken to a car and driven along a country road to the gateway of the Villa Belmonte. Here they were ordered out of the car and told to stand against a low wall, side by side. Mussolini moved forward heavily, stumbling. Claretta clung to his arm, tears running down her cheeks. As they turned to face the partisans, Audisio read aloud the death sentence pronounced upon Benito Mussolini, ex-dictator of Italy, by a partisan military court convened in Dongo.

There was a click as rifles were raised into position. Suddenly Claretta screamed, "No! No! Mussolini mustn't die!" She flung herself in front of him to protect him with her body.

Then a hail of fire cut them both down.

Reflecting later on the woman who died at Mussolini's side, Admiral Maugeri said, "She stood by him to the end and did not, like so many others, desert him in his dark and lonely hours of adversity. She could have fled to safety, but chose to die with him. There are many things that can be said against Clara Petacci, but this must be said for her: she was a brave and loyal woman."

Death was not the end for the fallen dictator. Eight years earlier he had expressed the hope that history would be impressed when the final curtain rang down on the melodrama that had been his life. "On my grave," he declared, "I want this epigraph: 'Here lies one of the most intelligent animals ever to appear on the surface of the earth.'" But four years before that he had prophesied more accurately in a biography of his brother Arnaldo, "It would be ingenuous of me to hope to be left in peace after death. Around the tombs of the leaders of revolutions there can be no peace."

The day following the execution the bodies of the couple were driven to the Piazzale Loreto in Milan and unloaded on top of seventeen other Fascist corpses. By 9:00 A.M. a huge mob of shouting, frenzied Milanese had gathered to scream curses at their dead leader. One woman fired five shots into Mussolini's body, shrieking, "That's for my five dead sons!" A man mockingly put a long stick in his hand as though it were a scepter. Two young Italians kicked him in the face.

To drive back the growing, uncontrollable crowds, partisan guards had to fire over their heads and turn a water hose on the front ranks. One partisan tried to appease the mob by holding up the bodies one at a time, for the crowd to see.

"Higher!" voices protested. "We can't see back here!"

Both bodies were strung up by ropes tied around the ankles, and there they swayed heads down in the morning winds of Milan. The crowd fell strangely silent, staring in bemusement at the blacksmith's son from Dovia who had once made his father proud by attacking another little boy with a dagger of stone, and who had since learned how to ride a whirlwind of vengeance, violence and hatred to the stormy heights of world fame.

Il Duce had taught his people to hate with passion, and now they showed they had learned the lesson well. Perhaps his greatest mistake was forgetting the warning of Machiavelli, "The best fortress is to be found in the love of the people, for although you may have fortresses they will not save you if you are hated by the people."

Ironically, Mussolini had almost predicted his own fate thirteen years earlier when he observed, "Everyone dies the death befitting his character."

BIBLIOGRAPHY

Borghi, Armando. *Mussolini: Red and Black*. London: Wishart Books Limited, 1935.

Cheney, L. J. *A History of the Western World*. London: George Allen & Unwin Ltd., 1959.

Clifford, Alexander G. *The Conquest of North Africa, 1940–1943*. Boston: Little, Brown and Company, 1943.

Doenitz, Karl. *Memoirs*. Cleveland and New York: World Publishing Company.

Dombrowski, Roman. *Mussolini: Twilight and Fall*. New York: Roy Publishers, 1956.

Fermi, Laura. *Mussolini*. Boston: Little, Brown and Company, 1962.

Foley, Charles. *Commando Extraordinary*. New York: G. P. Putnam's Sons, 1955.

Gellhorn, Martha. *The Face of War*. New York: Simon and Schuster, 1959.

Goerlitz, Walter. *History of the German General Staff*. New York: Praeger, 1959.

Greenfield, Kent Roberts, editor. *Command Decisions*. (Department of the Army.) New York: Harcourt, Brace and Company, 1959.

Grigson, Geoffrey, and Gibbs-Smith, Charles Harvard, editors. *People*. New York: Hawthorne Books, Inc.

Hibbert, Christopher. *Il Duce*. Boston: Little, Brown and Company, 1962.

Kalckreuth, Dunbar von. *Three Thousand Years of Rome.* New York and London: Alfred A. Knopf, 1930.

Kalijarvi, Thorsten V., editor. *Fascism in Action.* (Legislative Reference Service of Library of Congress.) Washington: U. S. Goverenment Printing Office, 1947.

Kemechey, L. *"Il Duce."* London: Williams & Norgate, 1930.

Ludwig, Emil. *Talks With Mussolini.* Boston: Little, Brown and Company, 1933.

Maugeri, Admiral Franco. *From the Ashes of Disgrace.* New York: Reynal & Hitchcock, 1948.

Monelli, Paolo. *Mussolini.* New York: Vanguard Press, Inc.

Mussolini, Benito. *My Autobiography.* New York: Charles Scribner's Sons, 1928.

————. *The Fall of Mussolini.* New York: Farrar, Straus and Company, 1948.

Mussolini, Rachele. *My Life With Mussolini.* London: Robert Hale Limited, 1959.

Packard, Reynolds and Eleanor. *Balcony Empire.* New York: Oxford University Press, 1942.

Rhodes, Anthony. *D'Annunzio. The Poet as Superman.* New York: McDowell, Oblensky, Inc., 1959.

Sarfatti, Margherita G. *The Life of Benito Mussolini.* London: Thornton Butterworth, Ltd., 1925.

Seldes, George. *Sawdust Caesar.* New York and London: Harper & Brothers, 1935.

Shirer, William L. *The Rise and Fall of the Third Reich.* New York: Simon and Schuster, 1960.

Steinbeck, John. *Once There Was a War.* New York: The Viking Press, Inc., 1958.

Taylor, A. J. P. *The Origins of the Second World War.* New York: Atheneum Publishers, 1961.

Trevor-Roper, H. R. *The Last Days of Hitler.* New York: The Macmillan Company, 1947.

INDEX

Abyssinia. *See* Ethiopia

Addis Ababa, Abyssinia, 120, 123, 125, 149, 163

Africa, 36, 116, 118, 123, 124, 138, 147, 149, 154-157, 161-163

Albania, 104, 137, 147, 148

Alexandria, 154

Allies, the, 44, 46, 47, 52, 54, 115, 116, 126, 133, 134, 137, 138, 140, 141, 143, 144, 153, 156-159, 162, 163, 168-170, 172, 176-178, 180, 181

Alps, 48, 144

Ambrosia, General, 159, 160, 164

Amendola, Deputy, 78, 81, 94, 95, 97

America, 18, 56, 58, 107, 112, 121, 127, 142, 143, 149, 153-155, 157, 162, 164, 172, 177, 183

Ancona, 42

Anschluss, 114, 131, 132, 133

Anti-Comintern Pact, 128

Anti-Semitism, 109, 110, 113, 114, 129, 143, 176

Apennines, 171

Arditi, 54, 56, 60

Assassination attempts, 100-102, 148

Atheism, 27, 71, 81, 103

Audisio, Walter, 183

Austria, 43, 44, 46-48, 51, 52

Austria-Hungary, 112-115, 121, 131, 132, 160

Avanti, 36, 40-44, 47, 55, 56

Aventino, 94, 95

Axis, the, 128, 131, 132, 134, 137, 141, 143, 153, 155, 157, 158, 160, 161, 175, 178

Badoglio, General, 120, 122, 123, 145, 146, 148, 155, 158, 160, 164, 167-172, 175

Balabanoff, Angelica, 29, 30, 31, 36, 40, 41, 44

Balbo, Italo, 54, 65, 66, 145

Balilla, 98, 99, 103

Balkans, 147, 148

Belgium, 145, 146

Berlin, 112, 128-131, 137, 143, 149, 172, 183

Berne, 28, 30, 31

Bianchi, Michele, 54, 65

Bissolati, Leonida, 39, 40

Blackshirts, 55, 56, 60-70, 72, 73, 80, 81, 87-91, 95, 98, 110, 130, 167, 179

Bologna, 44, 52, 63, 64, 66

Campo Imperatore, 171, 172

Caneva, 33

Caporetto, 51, 52, 57

Carso, the, 48, 49

Casablanca, 158

Catholicism, 12, 27, 28, 39, 57, 71, 80, 102-104, 108, 110

Catholic Party, 53, 61-64, 75, 76, 103

Cavallero, Marshal Ugo, 155, 159

Central Powers, 43, 44, 46, 52

Chamberlain, Neville, 127, 133-141

Cheka, Fascist, 72, 73, 80, 81, 87, 88, 90-92, 95, 101, 104, 107, 108, 110

Chiasso, 23, 31

Chicago Tribune, 97

Child, Richard Washburn, 72, 107

Churchill, Winston, 149, 152, 158, 160, 175

Ciano, Count Galeazzo, 105, 106, 110-112, 116, 125, 126, 130-132, 136, 137, 140, 141, 143-146, 148, 150, 154, 158, 161, 164-166, 175, 177, 178

Colonies, 16, 18, 37, 86, 104, 116, 122, 123, 147

About the Author

JULES ARCHER was born on January 27, 1915 in New York City, attended DeWitt Clinton High School and The City College of New York. His writing career began at the age of six, although it took fifteen years before an editor bought his material. Since then he has sold over a thousand stories and articles, as well as six books, which have been translated into twelve languages, adapted for television and included in many anthologies. Mr. Archer and his family now live in Pine Plains, New York.